The Joy of Squash
From acorn to zucchini

by Theresa Millang

Adventure Publications, Inc.
Cambridge, Minnesota

A special thank you goes to all who contributed to this cookbook.

Edited by Dan Downing

Book and cover design by Lora Westberg

10 9 8 7 6 5 4 3 2 1

Copyright 2013 by Theresa Nell Millang
Published by Adventure Publications, Inc.
820 Cleveland Street South
Cambridge, Minnesota 55008
1-800-678-7006
www.adventurepublications.net
Printed in China
ISBN: 978-1-59193-412-7

Table of Contents

SIDES

BARS & COOKIES

JAM & JELLY

PICKLES & CONDIMENTS

ABOUT THE AUTHOR

Introduction

Squash is native to the Americas and was a mainstay in the diets of many Native Americans for at least 5000 years. Early European settlers learned to value squash, especially for its ability to store through the winter. George Washington and Thomas Jefferson were avid squash growers. Since then, many new varieties have been brought here from all over the Americas, resulting in the various colors, shapes and sizes available today.

Squash are commonly divided into two groups: summer and winter. Summer squash are picked while still young and thin-skinned; they are tender and have a short storage life. Winter squash are harvested after they are fully mature and have developed a hard rind. Winter squash can keep for months, even into the winter, as the name implies.

The most common varieties of summer squash are zucchini, yellow crookneck, yellow straight neck, chayote and patty pan. Summer squash provides antioxidant nutrients, including carotenoids and lutein. It's an excellent source of vitamin C and also a good source of potassium, folate, and vitamins B2, K and A, as well as other healthy nutrients.

The most common varieties of winter squash include acorn, butternut, buttercup, spaghetti, Hubbard and banana, and also pumpkins. Winter squash is high in vitamins A, B2, B6 and C, and is a good source of potassium and fiber and other healthy nutrients. Pumpkin is a very nutritious food and offers many health benefits. Pumpkin is low in fat and rich in disease-fighting nutrients such as alpha-carotene, beta-carotene, fiber, vitamins C and E, potassium, magnesium and pantothenic acid.

California, Florida and Michigan lead the nation in commercial squash production. Many people grow squash in their backyard gardens; I grow squash in my garden every year.

The squash used in the recipes include: acorn, banana, buttercup, butternut, chayote, crookneck yellow, cucuzza, delicata, goldbar, Hubbard, patty pan, pumpkin, spaghetti, sugar pumpkin, turban and zucchini.

I have included all my favorite recipes, along with recipes from across the country. I hope you will try several. Grow squash in your garden . . . you will be amazed!

Selection and Storage

SUMMER SQUASH

Summer squash are thin-skinned and bruise easily. They hit their peak from early to late summer. Look for small to medium-size squash with brightly colored skin. Avoid squash with soft spots, dents or bruises in the skin. Summer squash is highly perishable. Store it in a plastic bag in the refrigerator for up to five days. Avoid storing squash near apples or avocados, as they release ethylene gas, which can discolor zucchini and other dark green squash and cause them to decay.

WINTER SQUASH

Winter squash have hard, thick rinds. This thick skin helps them store very well. Winter squash will stay fresh in cool, dark places for one to three months. When harvesting winter squash for storage, leave a portion of the stem attached to the squash. This helps the squash retain moisture.

EQUIVALENTS

Summer Squash
1 pound fresh = 3½ cups sliced or 2 cups grated
2 cups sliced and cooked = about 3 medium

Winter Squash
1 pound uncooked peeled squash = 1 cup cooked, mashed
1 pound squash = 2 to 3 servings
2½ pounds whole squash = about 3 cups pureed
12 ounces frozen squash = 1½ cups

Growing Squash

Both summer and winter squash will grow best in sunny areas with well-drained fertile soil. Organic matter can be added by incorporating compost into the soil. Mulching can increase yields in some varieties that have shallow roots.

Plant seeds anytime after the danger of frost has passed, from early spring until midsummer. Sow 4–5 seeds per hill, about 1 inch deep. Thin plants to 2–3 per hill.

Hills and rows of summer squash should be spaced about 3–4 feet apart. Winter squash hills and rows should be spaced about 4–5 feet apart.

Harvest summer squash often, picking the young ones before the seeds have fully ripened and while rinds are still soft. Winter squash should not be harvested until fully mature.

Cucumber beetles are a major pest, attacking seedlings, vines, and both immature and mature fruits. They can be controlled with an insecticide applied weekly, either as a spray or dust. Powdery mildew and bacterial wilt can cause problems. These can be treated with conventional or organic products. Consult your local nursery for recommendations.

Appetizers

Baked Zucchini Spears

Yes, recipe can be doubled!

2 small zucchinis, cut into 3½x½-inch strips

¼ cup all-purpose flour
3 tablespoons yellow cornmeal
½ teaspoon garlic powder
½ teaspoon chili powder
½ teaspoon paprika
½ teaspoon ground black pepper
¼ teaspoon salt
1 egg white, beaten in a small bowl
Cooking spray

Salsa or ketchup

Preheat oven to 425°. Grease a baking sheet.

Mix flour, cornmeal and seasonings in a shallow container. Dip zucchini strips into egg white, then into flour mixture. Place on greased baking sheet. Spray with cooking spray. Bake, turning once, until golden brown, about 20 minutes. Serve warm with salsa or ketchup. Refrigerate leftovers.

Makes 2 servings.

One serving contains approximately: Calories 100, Fat 1g, Carbohydrates 20g, Protein 4g

Cheddar Zucchini Bites

A tasty appetizer for that party!

3 cups thinly sliced zucchini
1 cup all-purpose baking mix, such as Bisquick
½ cup chopped yellow onion
½ teaspoon salt
¼ teaspoon ground black pepper
4 eggs, beaten
½ cup shredded mild Cheddar cheese
½ cup cooking oil
2 cloves garlic, finely chopped
1 tablespoon chopped parsley

Preheat oven to 350°. Grease a 13x9-inch baking dish.

Stir all ingredients together in a large bowl. Pour mixture into prepared baking dish.

Bake until bubbly and golden brown, about 25 minutes. Remove from oven; cut into bite-size pieces. Serve. Refrigerate leftovers.

Makes 36 servings.

One serving contains approximately: Calories 60, Fat 5g, Carbohydrates 3g, Protein 1.5g

Grilled Zucchini Bruschetta

Yellow summer squash may be used in place of zucchini, if desired.

1 10-ounce sourdough bread baguette, cut diagonally into 20 slices
½ cup balsamic vinaigrette salad dressing
1 small zucchini, cut lengthwise into 10 slices, then cut crosswise
   in half
20 fresh basil leaves
5 large fresh plum tomatoes, sliced lengthwise into 4 slices each
1⅓ cups light shredded mozzarella cheese

Heat grill to medium heat.

Brush bread with salad dressing on both sides. Place zucchini on bread. Top with remaining ingredients.

Grill until cheese is melted, about 8 minutes. Serve. Refrigerate leftovers.

Makes 10 servings.

One serving contains approximately: Calories 75, Fat 1.5g, Carbohydrates 11g, Protein 4g

Italian Cottage Dip with Zucchini

Offer assorted crackers along with the vegetable dippers.

1 16-ounce container low-fat cottage cheese
2 tablespoons milk
2 envelopes Italian dressing mix

2 small, firm zucchinis, quartered lengthwise, then halved crosswise
2 stalks crisp celery, halved lengthwise, then cut into 3-inch sticks
1 fresh carrot, peeled and cut into thin sticks

Blend cottage cheese and milk in a blender until smooth. Spoon into a medium serving bowl. Stir in salad dressing mix. Cover and chill before serving.

Serve dip with fresh zucchini, celery and carrot sticks. Refrigerate leftovers.

Makes 18 2-tablespoon servings.

One serving contains approximately: Calories 21, Fat 0.5g, Carbohydrates 65g, Protein 3g

Spicy Pumpkin Seeds

Snack on these zesty seeds along with other appetizers.

2 cups fresh pumpkin seeds
1 tablespoon butter or margarine, melted
1 teaspoon Worcestershire sauce
1 teaspoon granulated sugar
½ teaspoon salt
¼ teaspoon garlic powder
⅛ teaspoon ground red pepper

Preheat oven to 250°.

Line a rimmed baking sheet with aluminum baking foil; lightly grease foil.

Mix all ingredients in a small bowl until seeds are coated.

Spread pumpkin seeds onto prepared baking sheet. Bake, stirring often, until seeds are dry and lightly browned, about 1 hour. Remove from oven. Cool completely. Serve. Store covered in a plastic food container.

Makes 4 servings.

One serving contains approximately: Calories 95, Fat 5g, Carbohydrates 9g, Protein 3g

Soups

Acorn Squash Soup

Serve with crunchy breadsticks.

1 4-pound acorn squash cut in half, seeds discarded, baked

½ cup butter
½ cup finely chopped yellow onion
2 teaspoons finely chopped fresh garlic
¼ cup all-purpose flour
2 cups whole milk
1 14-ounce can chicken broth
⅓ cup maple syrup
¾ teaspoon salt
⅛ teaspoon ground red pepper
¾ cup heavy cream
1 tablespoon chopped fresh cilantro

1½ teaspoons chopped fresh basil leaves or ½ teaspoon dried basil leaves
1½ teaspoons chopped fresh oregano leaves or ½ teaspoon dried oregano leaves

½ cup sour cream mixed with 3 tablespoons chopped fresh cilantro

Remove baked squash pulp from skin. Place half of pulp in a food processor with a metal blade. Process on high speed until well mixed (should have about 4 cups).

Melt butter in a large saucepan. Add onion and garlic; cook and stir over medium heat 5 minutes. Stir in flour; cook and stir 4 minutes. Stir in milk and broth until smooth. Stir in squash, syrup, salt and red pepper. Gradually whisk in cream, cilantro, basil and oregano. Reduce heat to low, and heat until just warm; do not boil.

Top warm soup with sour cream mixture when serving. Refrigerate leftovers.

Makes 10 servings.

One serving contains approximately: Calories 320, Fat 20g, Carbohydrates 34g, Protein 5g

Butternut Squash Soup

This classic soup is always a favorite.

2 tablespoons extra virgin olive oil
1 cup diced carrots
½ cup diced celery
1 cup diced yellow onion
4 cups peeled and cubed butternut squash
½ teaspoon chopped fresh thyme
6 cups low-sodium chicken broth
Salt and ground black pepper to taste

Heat olive oil in a large soup pot. Add carrots, celery and onion; cook and stir over medium heat, about 4 minutes.

Add squash, thyme, broth, salt and pepper. Bring mixture to a boil. Reduce heat; simmer until squash is fork tender, about 30 minutes. Cool slightly, and puree soup in a blender or use an immersion blender to puree soup in soup pot. Serve. Refrigerate leftovers.

Makes 6 servings.

One serving contains approximately: Calories 140, Fat 6g, Carbohydrates 22g, Protein 6g

Butternut Squash Soup with Pears and Bacon

Garnish soup with chopped fresh thyme. Serve with crisp cheese breadsticks.

6 strips bacon

1 small yellow onion, chopped
4 cups peeled, seeded and cubed butternut squash
2 large ripe pears, peeled, cored and cubed
1 large stalk celery, chopped
2 14.5-ounce cans chicken broth

½ teaspoon dried thyme
½ teaspoon dried basil
½ cup half-and-half

Cook bacon in large stockpot until crisp; remove from pot. Drain on paper towels, crumble and set aside. Drain all but 1 tablespoon bacon grease from pot.

Add onion; cook and stir until browned. Add squash, pears, celery and chicken broth. Bring to a boil, then reduce heat. Cover and simmer 30 minutes. Let cool slightly; place in a blender or food processor and puree until smooth. Return to pot.

Stir in thyme, basil and bacon; simmer 10 minutes. Stir in half-and-half just to warm, do not boil. Serve warm. Refrigerate leftovers.

Makes 8 servings.

One serving contains approximately: Calories 180, Fat 11g, Carbohydrates 15g, Protein 6g

Cajun Zucchini Gumbo Soup

Gumbo soup is different than gumbo. Gumbo requires a roux. Both are delicious.

1 tablespoon cooking oil
1 pound boneless skinless chicken breast cut into 2-inch pieces
12 ounces Italian sausage links, cut into 1-inch pieces

3 cups cold water
½ cup uncooked long grain rice
1 large yellow onion, thinly sliced
1 28-ounce can whole tomatoes, including juice, cut-up
1 14-ounce can chicken broth
½ cup sliced fresh okra
1 tablespoon coarsely chopped flat leaf parsley
½ teaspoon salt
½ teaspoon dried thyme leaves
½ teaspoon finely chopped fresh garlic
¼ teaspoon coarse ground black pepper
⅛ teaspoon ground red pepper, such as cayenne

2 cups ¼-inch-thick sliced fresh zucchini

Heat cooking oil in a large soup pot. Add chicken and sausage; cook and stir over medium-high heat until browned, about 8 minutes. Drain fat. Stir in remaining ingredients except zucchini. Reduce heat to medium. Cook, stirring occasionally, until rice is tender, about 30 minutes.

Add zucchini; continue cooking until tender, about 6 minutes. Serve warm. Refrigerate leftovers.

Makes 6 servings.

One serving contains approximately: Calories 310, Fat 12g, Carbohydrates 23g, Protein 31g

Creamy Butternut Squash Soup

Cream cheese is the star ingredient in this good soup.

¼ cup butter or margarine
½ cup finely chopped yellow onion

3 cups water
6 cups peeled and cubed butternut squash
6 teaspoons chicken bouillon granules
½ teaspoon dried tarragon, optional
½ teaspoon ground white pepper

2 8-ounce packages cream cheese, cubed

Melt butter in a soup pot. Add onion; stir and cook over medium heat until soft.

Add water, squash, bouillon, tarragon and pepper. Bring mixture to a boil, then reduce heat and simmer until squash is tender, about 20 minutes. Cool slightly. Puree mixture, in batches, with cream cheese in a food processor until smooth. Return soup to pot, and heat until warm. Serve. Refrigerate leftovers.

Makes 6 servings.

One serving contains approximately: Calories 397, Fat 35g, Carbohydrates 22g, Protein 7g

Crock Pot Butternut Squash Soup

Top this creamy butternut squash soup with cheese-flavored croutons.

2 tablespoons margarine
½ cup chopped yellow onion
1 (2-pound) butternut squash, peeled, seeded and cubed
2 cups water
½ teaspoon dried marjoram leaves or dried basil leaves
⅛ teaspoon ground nutmeg
¼ teaspoon ground black pepper
⅛ teaspoon ground red pepper (cayenne)
4 chicken bouillon cubes

1 8-ounce package cream cheese, cubed

Melt margarine in a nonstick small saucepan. Add onions; cook and stir until tender, about 4 minutes. Remove from heat; set aside.

In a 3- to 4-quart crock pot, mix onions and remaining ingredients except cream cheese.

Cover; cook on low heat setting 6–8 hours.

Place one-half the mixture in a food processor at a time. Cover and process until smooth. Return mixture to crock pot. Stir in cream cheese. Cover; cook on low heat setting about 30 minutes longer or until cheese is melted, stirring until smooth. Serve warm. Refrigerate leftovers.

Makes 6 servings.

One serving contains approximately: Calories 231, Fat 17g, Carbohydrates 15g, Protein 5g

Crookneck Yellow Squash and Corn Soup

Summer squash and corn make a delicious starter soup.

1 tablespoon extra virgin olive oil
1 medium shallot, chopped
2 medium-size crookneck yellow squash, diced (about 1 pound)
1 tablespoon chopped fresh oregano
1 14-ounce can reduced-sodium chicken broth or vegetable broth
¼ teaspoon salt
1 cup fresh corn kernels (about 1 large ear)
1 teaspoon fresh lemon juice

¼ cup crumbled feta cheese
2 teaspoons chopped fresh thyme or fresh oregano leaves, divided

Heat olive oil in a large saucepan over medium heat. Add shallot; cook and stir 1 minute. Add squash and 1 teaspoon fresh herbs; cook and stir until squash is soft, about 5 minutes. Place mixture in a blender and process until smooth. Return mixture to saucepan. Stir in corn; simmer until corn is tender, about 5 minutes. Remove from heat. Stir in lemon juice.

Serve topped with feta cheese and remaining fresh herbs. Refrigerate leftovers.

Makes 4 1-cup servings.

One serving contains approximately: Calories 115, Fat 6g, Carbohydrates 14g, Protein 5g

Curried Winter Squash Soup

Serve warm soup along with bread, cheese and a salad for a tasty lunch.

2 tablespoons butter or margarine
6 green onions, finely chopped
2 cloves fresh garlic, minced
1 small green bell pepper, cored, seeded and finely chopped
¼ cup minced fresh flat leaf parsley
2 teaspoons minced fresh basil or 1 teaspoon dried basil, crumbled
2 pounds butternut squash, peeled, seeded and cubed
1 14.5-ounce can plum tomatoes with juice
4 cups canned chicken broth
½ teaspoon ground allspice
¼ teaspoon ground mace
Pinch of ground nutmeg
2 teaspoons curry powder
1 ham bone or ½ pound smoked ham
¼ teaspoon each: salt, black pepper

Melt butter in a large saucepan over medium heat. Add onion, garlic, bell pepper, parsley and basil. Cook and stir 5 minutes. Stir in squash, tomatoes, broth, allspice, mace and nutmeg. Add ham bone. Bring to a boil, then reduce heat to low. Cover and simmer 50–60 minutes or until squash is very tender. Discard ham bone.

Strain the liquid through a sieve into a large saucepan. Place the solids in a food processor. Add 1 cup strained liquid to solids in food processor. Puree until smooth. Pour puree back into the saucepan. Stir in curry powder. Bring to a boil, then reduce heat to low; simmer 10 minutes. Stir in salt and pepper. Serve. Refrigerate leftovers up to 3 days.

Makes 6 servings.

One serving contains approximately: Calories 192, Fat 6g, Carbohydrates 22g, Protein 15g

Favorite Pumpkin Soup

Use fresh pumpkin puree instead of canned, if desired.

¼ cup butter
⅓ cup finely chopped yellow onion
½ cup finely chopped celery
½ cup finely chopped carrot
1 tablespoon minced shallots
4 cups canned pumpkin puree (not pie mix)
2 cups chicken broth
1½ cups water

¼ teaspoon dried thyme leaves
½ cup heavy cream
¼ teaspoon ground black pepper
Salt to taste

1 small French baguette cut into ¼-inch slices
5 tablespoons blue cheese crumbles

Melt butter in a soup pot. Add onion, celery, carrot and shallots; cook and stir over medium heat 3 minutes. Add pumpkin puree, broth and water. Cook over medium heat until vegetables are tender. Remove from heat. Puree mixture in a food processor or blender. Return to saucepan. Stir in thyme, cream, black pepper and salt. Heat mixture until warm, but do not boil.

Place bread slices on a baking sheet; broil until crispy. Remove from oven; sprinkle with cheese. Serve over the warm soup. Refrigerate leftovers.

Makes 5 servings.

One serving contains approximately: Calories 250, Fat 20g, Carbohydrates 22g, Protein 5g

Garden Tomato and Zucchini Soup

This is a delicious way to use the abundant tomatoes from the garden.

3 tablespoons extra virgin olive oil
2 cups cubed zucchini
2 cloves fresh garlic, minced

8 large ripe tomatoes, cored
½ cup chopped yellow onion
1 tablespoon chopped fresh red chile pepper

1 14-ounce can vegetable broth
1 tablespoon dried tarragon
2 teaspoons dried dill weed
1 teaspoon salt
¼ teaspoon ground black pepper

Heat olive oil in a skillet over medium heat. Add zucchini and garlic. Stir and cook 3 minutes. Remove from heat; set aside.

Process tomatoes, onion and chile pepper in a food processor until almost pureed but leaving small chunks. Place mixture in a soup pot. Add vegetable broth, dried herbs, salt and black pepper. Bring mixture to a boil. Reduce heat to low. Add zucchini and garlic mixture to pot. Cover and simmer 45 minutes. Serve. Refrigerate leftovers.

Makes 8 servings.

One serving contains approximately: Calories 90, Fat 5g, Carbohydrates 11g, Protein 2g

Hubbard Squash Soup

Garnish with toasted shelled pumpkin seeds instead of hazelnuts, if desired.

1 6-pound Hubbard squash, halved lengthwise, seeds discarded
3 tablespoons extra virgin olive oil
3 large cloves fresh garlic, peeled and mashed
1½ teaspoons dried sage
½ teaspoon dried thyme

2 tablespoons butter
1 large leek, halved lengthwise then thinly sliced crosswise
2 carrots, peeled and diced

5 cups low-sodium chicken broth
1 bay leaf
1 teaspoon salt
2 teaspoons fresh lemon juice
Freshly ground black pepper to taste

½ cup hazelnuts, toasted, skinned and chopped
2 tablespoons snipped fresh chives
Pinch of cayenne

Preheat oven to 400°. Line a rimmed baking sheet with parchment paper.

Mix olive oil, garlic, sage and thyme in a small bowl until well blended. Spread the mixture on the flesh side of squash. Put squash cut-side down on prepared baking sheet. Bake until tender, about 1 hour. Remove from oven; cool squash cut-side up. Scrape out flesh from rind (should have about 5 cups).

Melt butter in a soup pot over medium heat. Add leeks and carrots; cook and stir 10 minutes. Add squash, broth, bay leaf and salt. Bring mixture to a boil over high heat. Reduce heat to low; cover and simmer 30 minutes. Remove bay leaf. Cool soup slightly. Puree mixture in batches in a blender. Return soup to pot. Stir in lemon juice. Season to taste with black pepper, and add more salt if needed. Garnish each serving with nuts, chives and just a pinch of cayenne. Refrigerate leftovers.

Makes 10 servings.

One serving contains approximately: Calories 244, Fat 14g, Carbohydrates 29g, Protein 9g

Smoky Tomato Butternut Squash Soup

The sun-dried tomatoes add a delicious flavor to this soup.

2 tablespoons butter
1 medium-size yellow onion, chopped
3 cups peeled and cubed butternut squash
2 ribs celery, sliced

1 32-ounce container chicken or vegetable stock
1 28-ounce can crushed tomatoes
½ cup smoked sun-dried tomatoes, chopped

1½ teaspoons dried basil
¼ teaspoon salt or to taste
Smokehouse pepper to taste

Melt butter in a large soup pot. Add onion and squash; cook and stir over medium heat 10 minutes. Add celery; cook and stir 5 minutes.

Add stock and tomatoes to pot. Bring mixture to a boil; reduce heat. Cover and simmer 35 minutes. Cool slightly. Transfer to a blender; puree until smooth. Return to soup pot. Add basil, salt and pepper; simmer 10 minutes. Serve. Refrigerate leftovers.

Makes 8 servings.

One serving contains approximately: Calories 170, Fat 5g, Carbohydrates 28g, Protein 7g

Spaghetti Squash Vegetable Soup

Serve a cup of this vegetarian soup with cheese breadsticks.

1 2-pound spaghetti squash, halved and seeds removed

1 tablespoon cooking oil
2 8-ounce packages cleaned and cut mirepoix, or clean and
  cut 1 pound total of onions, carrots and celery
3 cloves fresh garlic, minced
1 10-ounce package baby bella mushrooms, quartered
1 28-ounce can roma tomatoes with basil
2 32-ounce cartons vegetable stock
1½ tablespoons minced fresh thyme
Salt and black pepper to taste
1 6-ounce package baby spinach, chopped

Place squash skin side up (one half at a time) on a microwave-safe dish; cover with microwave-safe plastic wrap. Microwave on high 10–12 minutes or until tender. Let stand until cool enough to handle, about 15 minutes. Carefully remove plastic food wrap to avoid steam. Loosen spaghetti strands with a fork; scoop out and set aside.

Heat oil in a large soup pot. Add mirepoix; cook and stir 3 minutes or until vegetables are softened. Add garlic and mushrooms; stir and cook 2 minutes. Stir in tomatoes; simmer 10 minutes. Add vegetable stock; simmer 20 minutes. Stir in cooked squash, thyme, salt and black pepper. Simmer 5 minutes. Stir in spinach until wilted, about 2 minutes. Serve. Refrigerate leftovers.

Makes 15 1-cup servings.

One serving contains approximately: Calories 80, Fat 2g, Carbohydrates 14g, Protein 2g

Spicy Winter Squash Soup

Serve this tasty spicy soup with crisp breadsticks.

2 tablespoons extra virgin olive oil
6 cloves fresh garlic, chopped
2 tablespoons grated ginger
1 jalapeno pepper, seeded and finely chopped
1 tablespoon salt
¼ teaspoon cayenne pepper

4 pounds butternut squash, peeled, seeded and cut into 2-inch cubes
3 cups chicken broth
1 tablespoon light brown sugar
3 cups cold water
3 tablespoons heavy whipping cream

Heat olive oil in a 5-quart stockpot over high heat. Add garlic, ginger, jalapeno and salt. Cook, stirring constantly, for 1 minute; do not brown. Add cayenne; stir and cook 30 seconds.

Add squash, chicken broth, brown sugar and water. Bring mixture to a boil. Reduce heat and simmer, stirring occasionally, until squash is tender, about 20 minutes.

In a blender, puree soup in batches until smooth, then pour back into the stockpot. Stir in whipping cream. Adjust seasonings to taste if needed. Serve hot. Refrigerate leftovers.

Makes 6–8 servings.

One serving contains approximately: Calories 169, Fat 6g, Carbohydrates 30g, Protein 3g

Summer Squash Polenta Soup

Quick-cooking polenta is used in this good soup.

1 tablespoon cooking oil
1 cup coarsely chopped yellow squash
1 cup coarsely chopped zucchini
1 cup peeled and coarsely chopped carrots
1 cup chopped yellow onion

6 cups reduced-sodium chicken broth or vegetable broth
2 cups fresh chopped tomatoes
1 6-ounce can tomato paste
1 tablespoon dried basil

¼ cup quick-cooking polenta
3 cups coarsely chopped spinach or Swiss chard
Garlic salt to taste

Heat cooking oil in a large stockpot over medium-high heat. Add yellow squash, zucchini, carrots and onion; cook and stir until lightly browned.

Stir in broth, tomatoes, tomato paste and basil; bring to a boil. Reduce heat, cover and simmer 30 minutes.

Stir in polenta; cook 5 minutes. Stir in spinach or Swiss chard and season to taste with garlic salt. Serve. Refrigerate leftovers.

Makes 4–6 servings.

One serving contains approximately: Calories 150, Fat 4g, Carbohydrates 27g, Protein 5g

Turkey Butternut Squash Soup

Serve this good soup with warm cornbread . . . buttered of course.

1 tablespoon cooking oil
2 leeks, trimmed, chopped and rinsed
1 red bell pepper, chopped
3 cloves fresh garlic, minced
4 cups reduced-sodium chicken broth
1½ pounds butternut squash, peeled, seeded and cut into 1-inch cubes
2 teaspoons dried thyme leaves
1½ teaspoons ground cumin

1 pound turkey cutlets, cut into ½x2-inch strips
2 cups frozen corn kernels
2 tablespoons fresh lime juice
½ teaspoon crushed red pepper
¼ teaspoon salt, or to taste
¼ teaspoon freshly ground black pepper, or to taste

Heat cooking oil in a Dutch oven over medium-high heat. Add leeks and red bell pepper; cook and stir until vegetables begin to soften, about 4 minutes. Add garlic; cook and stir 1 minute. Stir in broth, squash, thyme and cumin. Cover and bring mixture to a boil. Reduce heat to medium-low and cook until vegetables are tender, about 10 minutes.

Add turkey and corn. Return to a simmer and cook until turkey is just cooked through, about 5 minutes. Stir in lime juice, crushed red pepper, salt and black pepper to taste. Serve. Refrigerate leftovers.

Makes 24 servings.

Variation: Add diced leftover turkey the last 10 minutes of cooking time.

One serving contains approximately: Calories 231, Fat 3g, Carbohydrates 31g, Protein 6g

Salads

Acorn Squash and Beet Salad

Serve with assorted crisp crackers.

6 cups coarsely chopped romaine lettuce
1 cup coarsely grated acorn squash
1 cup cooked and peeled fresh beets, julienne-cut

¼ cup extra virgin olive oil
2 tablespoons white balsamic vinegar
1 tablespoon pure maple syrup
Salt and pepper to taste

⅓ cup crumbled smoky blue cheese
⅓ cup chopped walnuts, toasted

Layer lettuce, squash and beets in 4 salad bowls.

Whisk olive oil, vinegar, syrup, salt and pepper in a small container; drizzle over salads.

Top each salad equally with cheese and walnuts. Serve. Refrigerate leftovers.

Makes 4 servings.

One serving contains approximately: Calories 290, Fat 24g, Carbohydrates 17g, Protein 6g

Butternut Squash-Kale Salad

Serve this tasty nutritious salad for a special lunch.

1 pound fresh kale, stems removed, leaves sliced
1 cup vegetable broth, divided
1 2-pound butternut squash, peeled, seeded
   and cut into ½-inch cubes

1 red onion, slivered
4 pitted dates, finely chopped
2 tablespoons wine vinegar

Place kale and ½ cup vegetable broth in a large pot. Cover and cook over medium heat, stirring frequently, until kale is wilted, about 3 minutes. Add squash and continue cooking, stirring occasionally, until both are tender but not mushy, about 10 minutes. Place in a large bowl; cool to room temperature.

Mix ½ cup vegetable broth, onion, dates and vinegar in a small saucepan. Bring to a boil, then lower heat and simmer uncovered until onion is very tender and liquid reduced by half, about 6 minutes. Cool and add to bowl with squash mixture; toss. Serve at room temperature. Refrigerate leftovers.

Makes 8 servings.

Variation: Add chickpeas or black beans.

One serving contains approximately: Calories 100, Fat (trace amount), Carbohydrates 24g, Protein 3g

Butternut Squash Panzanella Salad

Butternut squash is a delicious addition to this colorful bread salad.

4 cups 1-inch cubed peeled
   butternut squash
5 tablespoons extra virgin
   olive oil, divided
3 tablespoons capers, drained
1 tablespoon chopped fresh garlic
¼ teaspoon ground black pepper

4 cups 1-inch cubed hearty
   crusty bread
1½ teaspoons chopped fresh sage
¼ teaspoon salt, or to taste

½ teaspoon freshly grated lemon zest
2 tablespoons fresh lemon juice
1 tablespoon red wine vinegar
Salt and ground black pepper to taste

4 cups coarsely chopped
   romaine lettuce
Half of a small red onion, thinly sliced
Feta cheese

Preheat oven to 375°. Lightly grease 2 large baking sheets.

Toss squash, 1 tablespoon olive oil, capers, garlic, and black pepper in a large bowl; place mixture on one prepared baking sheet. Bake until squash is tender, about 30 minutes. Remove from oven and cool.

Toss bread, 1 tablespoon olive oil, sage and salt in the same bowl; place on the second prepared baking sheet. Bake until toasted and golden brown, about 10 minutes, tossing halfway through baking time. Remove from oven and cool.

In a large bowl, whisk lemon zest, lemon juice, vinegar, 3 tablespoons olive oil, salt and pepper to taste. Add lettuce, onion, cooled squash, cooled bread; toss. Serve on salad plates; sprinkle with feta. Serve immediately. Refrigerate leftovers.

Makes 4 servings.

One serving contains approximately: Calories 290, Fat 17g, Carbohydrates 32g, Protein 6g

Chayote and Avocado Salad

Serve with crisp crackers.

3 chayote squash, pitted and diced
1 cup sliced radishes
1 ripe avocado, peeled, pitted and sliced
⅓ cup sliced green onions
1 2¼-ounce can sliced black olives, drained

⅓ cup spicy ranch salad dressing
1 tablespoon cider vinegar

Place squash, radishes, avocado, onions and olives in a large bowl.

Stir salad dressing and vinegar in a small container; drizzle over salad in bowl.
Toss to coat.

Makes 6 servings.

One serving contains approximately: Calories 140, Fat 11g, Carbohydrates 10g, Protein 2g

Couscous Salad with Zucchini and Black Beans

Couscous is so convenient to use for quick meals.

1½ cups water
1 cup whole wheat couscous

1 medium-size zucchini, finely chopped
2 fresh tomatoes, chopped
1 red bell pepper, chopped
2 green onions, sliced
1 cup fresh corn kernels
¼ cup chopped fresh cilantro
1 15-ounce can black beans, rinsed and drained
½ teaspoon chili powder, or to taste
¼ cup fresh lime juice
1 cup pepitas (pumpkin seeds)

Bring water to a boil in a medium-size saucepan. Stir in couscous; remove from heat. Cover and let stand 5 minutes, then fluff with a fork and transfer to a large bowl.

Add remaining ingredients to bowl. Mix until combined. Serve. Refrigerate leftovers.

Makes 8 servings.

One serving contains approximately: Calories 170, Fat 3g, Carbohydrates 32g, Protein 16g

Goldbar Squash Summertime Pasta Salad

Goldbar squash (a zucchini-type summer squash) is used in this pasta salad.

1 bunch asparagus, trimmed, cut in 1½-inch pieces
Half of a red bell pepper, cored and thinly sliced
1 medium-size unpeeled goldbar squash, cut into quarters,
   then cut into 1-inch pieces
1 medium-size unpeeled zucchini, cut into quarters,
   then cut into 1-inch pieces
1 16-ounce package uncooked spiral pasta

3 green onions, shredded
1 pint cherry tomatoes, halved
1 jar (6.7-ounce) Italian basil pesto sauce
Salt and black pepper to taste
Zest of 3 fresh lemons
½ cup fresh lemon juice
⅓ cup shredded Parmesan or Romano cheese

Blanch asparagus in a large pot of boiling water 1 minute. Add bell pepper, goldbar squash and zucchini; blanch 30 seconds. Remove from water and place in a bowl of ice water 30 seconds. Drain well and place in a large bowl.

Return water to a boil. Add pasta and cook following package directions. Drain; rinse with cold water. Add cooked pasta, green onions, tomatoes and pesto sauce to the mixture in the large bowl; toss. Season with salt and pepper to taste. Add lemon zest, lemon juice and cheese to large bowl; toss until combined. Serve. Refrigerate leftovers.

Makes 12 servings.

One serving contains approximately: Calories 260, Fat 11g, Carbohydrates 36g, Protein 6g

Grilled Squash and Chickpeas Salad

Grilled zucchini and yellow summer squash are featured in this summer salad.

2 tablespoons extra virgin olive oil
2 zucchini, thickly sliced lengthwise
2 yellow summer squash, thickly sliced lengthwise
1 yellow bell pepper, cored and quartered
1 red bell pepper, cored and quartered
1 small red onion cut into thick rings

2 cloves fresh garlic, chopped
2 tablespoons red wine vinegar
2 tablespoons chopped fresh basil leaves
1 15-ounce can chickpeas, rinsed and drained
Salt and black pepper to taste

½ cup grated Parmesan cheese

Rub olive oil on the grill grates, then preheat grill to medium-high heat.

Working in batches, grill zucchini, yellow squash, bell peppers and onion, turning once, until just charred in parts and tender, about 6 minutes. Remove and place on a baking sheet. Continue grilling remaining vegetables as before. Set grilled vegetables aside to cool, then cut into bite-size pieces and place in a large bowl.

Add all remaining ingredients except the cheese to bowl. Toss gently. Garnish with cheese and serve immediately. Refrigerate leftovers.

Makes 6 servings.

One serving contains approximately: Calories 230, Fat 9g, Carbohydrates 29g, Protein 10g

Tomato and Zucchini Pasta Salad

Serve with warm Italian bread . . . buttered of course.

8 ounces uncooked dried penne pasta

2 medium-size fresh tomatoes, cut into 1-inch pieces
2 cups ¼-inch sliced fresh zucchini
2 green onions, thinly sliced
1 cup ½-inch cubed Cheddar cheese or Jack cheese
½ cup Italian vinaigrette salad dressing
1 tablespoon chopped fresh oregano leaves
1 tablespoon chopped fresh basil leaves
1 tablespoon chopped fresh flat leaf parsley

Mixed lettuce leaves

Cook pasta following package directions. Rise with cold water then drain in a colander.

Transfer to a large bowl; add all remaining ingredients except lettuce leaves. Toss until coated. Cover and refrigerate 30 minutes. Serve on lettuce leaves. Refrigerate leftovers.

Makes 8 servings.

One serving contains approximately: Calories 240, Fat 12g, Carbohydrates 25g, Protein 8g

Zucchini-Veggie Slaw

Serve this good slaw with grilled hamburgers or hot dogs.

2 cups coarsely shredded unpeeled fresh zucchini, well drained
2 cups shredded green cabbage
1 medium-size carrot, peeled and shredded
2 green onions, thinly sliced
⅓ cup thinly sliced radishes

⅓ cup light mayonnaise
⅓ cup mild picante sauce
½ teaspoon ground cumin
¼ teaspoon ground black pepper, or to taste
Salt to taste

In a large bowl, mix together zucchini, cabbage, carrot, onion and radish.

Mix remaining ingredients in a small bowl; add to zucchini mixture and toss until coated. Cover and chill well before serving. Refrigerate leftovers.

Makes 8 servings.

Variation: Omit cumin. Use ⅓ cup zesty Italian dressing instead of picante sauce.

One serving contains approximately: Calories 59, Fat 3g, Carbohydrates 7g, Protein 1g

Meals

Acorn Squash with Sausage Stuffing

Serve this attractive dish with a side of sliced garden fresh tomatoes.

1 8.5-ounce package corn muffin mix

4 small acorn squash, halved lengthwise,
  seeds discarded
¼ teaspoon salt
¼ teaspoon ground black pepper

8 ounces bulk pork sausage
1 cup coarsely chopped
  yellow onion
1 cup sliced celery
3 cloves fresh garlic, minced
1 tablespoon snipped fresh sage
  or thyme
1 tablespoon butter, melted
½ cup chicken broth

Preheat oven to 400°.

Bake corn muffin mix following package directions for 8x8x2-inch baking pan.
Cool in pan, then cut into ¼-inch cubes; set aside.

Reduce heat to 350°. Lightly grease a 15x10x1-inch baking pan.

Sprinkle cavities of each squash half with salt and pepper; place cut-side down
on prepared baking pan. Bake uncovered until tender, about 30 minutes. Remove
from oven. Carefully turn squash cut-side up, leaving squash on baking pan.

Cook sausage, onion, celery and garlic in a extra large nonstick skillet until sausage is browned and vegetables tender; drain and discard fat. Stir in sage. Add
cornbread cubes; toss to combine. Drizzle with butter and broth; toss to moisten.
Spoon mixture equally into squash cavities. Bake uncovered 30 minutes or until
top is golden brown and mixture is heated through. Serve. Refrigerate leftovers.

Makes 8 servings.

One serving contains approximately: Calories 304, Fat 14g, Carbohydrates 38g, Protein 9g

Baked Acorn Squash with Pork Tenderloin Stuffing

Serve with a garden salad.

3 medium-size acorn squash, halved lengthwise, seeds removed
½ cup water
Salt and black pepper to taste

½ cup butter
¾ pound pork tenderloin cut into 2x½-inch strips
1 cup chopped yellow onion
1 large clove fresh garlic, finely chopped
1 cup ¼-inch sliced celery
½ teaspoon dried marjoram leaves
½ teaspoon dried thyme
½ teaspoon salt
¼ teaspoon black pepper

2 cups 1-inch cubed rye bread

Preheat oven to 375°.
Place squash cut-side up in a 13x9x2-inch baking pan; add ½ cup water. Cover with aluminum foil. Bake until fork tender, about 45 minutes. Remove from oven and sprinkle with salt and pepper to taste; keep warm.

Melt butter in a 10-inch nonstick skillet until hot. Add pork, onion, garlic, celery, marjoram, thyme, salt and pepper. Stir and cook over medium-high heat until pork is no longer pink, about 15 minutes.

Stir in bread until heated through. Spoon mixture evenly into each baked squash. Serve warm. Refrigerate leftovers.

Makes 6 servings.

One serving contains approximately: Calories 490, Fat 27g, Carbohydrates 44g, Protein 24g

Baked Rice with Sausage and Zucchini

Serve with a lettuce and tomato salad, dressed with zesty Italian dressing.

2 tablespoons extra virgin olive oil
12-ounces Italian sausage links, hot or sweet, cut into ½-inch slices
1 cup finely chopped yellow onion

1 small zucchini, halved lengthwise and thinly sliced
½ cup chopped green bell pepper
1 cup thinly sliced button mushrooms
3 cups long grain white rice
2¾ cups chicken broth
½ cup grated Parmesan cheese
1 tablespoon minced fresh basil or 1 teaspoon dried basil
¼ teaspoon salt or to taste
¼ teaspoon ground black pepper

Preheat oven to 350°. Grease a 2-quart baking dish.

Heat olive oil in a heavy 12-inch skillet over medium-high heat. Add sausage; stir and cook until browned. Remove from skillet; set aside. Drain all but 1 tablespoon fat from skillet. Add onion; cook and stir 5 minutes. Add zucchini, bell pepper and mushrooms; cook and stir 5 minutes. Stir in rice. Stir in broth; bring to a boil. Stir in Parmesan cheese, basil, salt and black pepper.

Spoon mixture into prepared baking dish. Cover and bake 25 minutes. Uncover and continue baking 10 minutes or until almost all the liquid has been absorbed, the rice is tender and top is slightly crusty. Serve warm. Refrigerate leftovers.

Makes 4 servings.

One serving contains approximately: Calories 605, Fat 33g, Carbohydrates 46g, Protein 30g

Baked Turkey Butternut Squash Skillet

Serve with a lettuce and tomato salad, along with crusty rolls.

¼ cup bread crumbs
¼ cup Parmesan cheese
2 tablespoons extra virgin olive oil, divided
1 small yellow onion, cut in half and thinly sliced
2 teaspoons butter
1 rib celery, thinly sliced
¾ pound turkey breast, cut into bite-size cubes
1 teaspoon dried thyme
2 cloves fresh garlic, minced
¼ teaspoon salt or to taste
¼ teaspoon ground black pepper
2 cups peeled butternut squash cubed into bite-size pieces

Preheat oven to 375°.

Mix together bread crumbs, Parmesan cheese and 1 tablespoon olive oil in a small bowl. Set aside.

Heat 1 tablespoon olive oil in an ovenproof skillet over medium heat. Add onion, butter and celery; cook and stir 5 minutes. Add turkey, thyme, garlic, salt and pepper; cook and stir until turkey is browned. Add squash; cook 5 minutes.

Top with bread crumb mixture. Cover skillet and bake in preheated oven until turkey is completely cooked, about 20 minutes. Serve. Refrigerate leftovers.

Makes 3 servings.

One serving contains approximately: Calories 320, Fat 14g, Carbohydrates 18g, Protein 30g

Baked Zucchini Chicken Casserole

Variation: Use yellow summer squash.

1 6-ounce package stuffing mix
¾ cup butter, melted

3 cups diced fresh zucchini
2 cups cubed cooked rotisserie chicken breast
1 10.75-ounce can undiluted condensed cream of chicken soup
1 fresh carrot, shredded
½ cup chopped yellow onion
½ cup dairy sour cream
¼ teaspoon salt
¼ teaspoon ground black pepper

Preheat oven to 350°. Grease a 2-quart baking dish.

Stir stuffing mix and butter in a large bowl; remove ½ cup mixture and set aside.
Add remaining ingredients to bowl; mix well.

Spoon mixture into prepared baking dish. Sprinkle top with reserved ½ cup stuffing
mixture. Bake uncovered until bubbly and golden brown, about 45 minutes.

Makes 6 servings.

Variation: Use yellow summer squash.

One serving contains approximately: Calories 482, Fat 31g, Carbohydrates 27g, Protein 20g

Bowtie Bake with Butternut Squash and Prosciutto

Rosemary and thyme flavor this special butternut squash casserole.

2 tablespoons extra virgin olive oil
1 medium-size red onion, chopped
2 tablespoons fresh rosemary, chopped
1 teaspoon chopped fresh thyme
8 slices prosciutto, torn into
   bite-size pieces
4 cups butternut squash,
   peeled and cubed

1 16-ounce box bowtie
   pasta (farfalle)
2 tablespoons butter
2 tablespoons all-purpose flour
2 cups half-and-half
1 teaspoon grated nutmeg
2 cups shredded mozzarella
   cheese, divided

Preheat oven to 350°. Lightly grease a 13x9-inch baking dish.

Heat olive oil in a medium-size nonstick saucepan over medium heat. Add onion, rosemary, thyme and prosciutto. Stir and cook until onion is soft, about 5 minutes. Remove from heat; set aside.

Blanch squash in boiling water until soft, about 5 minutes. Remove from pot and pat dry. Cook pasta in a large pot until tender but firm, following package directions. Drain well and return to pot.

Melt butter in a medium saucepan. Whisk in flour until smooth. Gradually whisk in half-and-half until smooth and just begins to bubble. Stir in nutmeg. Add onion mixture and squash to pasta in pot, then stir in sauce.

Place half the pasta mixture in prepared baking dish. Sprinkle with 1 cup cheese. Top with remaining pasta mixture and remaining cheese. Bake uncovered until golden brown, about 35 minutes. Serve hot. Refrigerate leftovers.

Makes 8 servings.

One serving contains approximately: Calories 481, Fat 21g, Carbohydrates 57g, Protein 20g

Bratwurst Kabobs

Hint: Remember, the potatoes have to be cooked . . . or just leave them out.

1 tablespoon butter
1 yellow onion, chopped
1 cup beer or non-alcoholic beer
2 tablespoons Dijon mustard
1 tablespoon brown sugar

1 19-ounce package fresh bratwurst, sliced diagonally, ½ inch thick
1 each: small red, yellow and orange bell peppers, cored and cut into
   1-inch pieces
2 zucchini, sliced ½ inch thick
2 yellow crookneck squash, sliced ½ inch thick
Half of a red onion, cut into 1-inch pieces
8 tiny red potatoes, cooked

Heat butter in a small saucepan. Add onions; cook and stir over low heat until soft, about 8 minutes. Add beer, mustard and sugar. Bring mixture to a boil, then reduce heat and simmer 5 minutes. Remove from heat and set aside.

Thread sausage and vegetables onto metal skewers.

Cook on a grill, over medium heat, for about 10–15 minutes, turning and basting with half the sauce mixture, until lightly charred and cooked through. Remove skewers from grill and place on a serving platter; pour remaining sauce over top. Serve. Refrigerate leftovers.

Makes 4 servings.

One serving contains approximately: Calories 350, Fat 27g, Carbohydrates 10g, Protein 18g

Chicken with Zucchini Pasta Skillet

Serve with a lettuce and cucumber salad with Italian salad dressing.

2 cups uncooked dried rotini pasta

2 tablespoons extra virgin olive oil
1 small yellow onion, thinly sliced
2 cloves fresh garlic, chopped
2 cups 1-inch cubed unpeeled
   fresh zucchini
1 cup small fresh broccoli florets
1 large red or green bell
   pepper, chopped

1 pound boneless skinless cooked
   rotisserie chicken breast cut into
   bite-size pieces
¼ cup Italian salad dressing,
   or to taste
Salt and black pepper to taste

¼ cup grated Parmesan cheese

Cook pasta following package directions; drain and set aside.

Heat olive oil in a large nonstick skillet over medium-high heat. Add onion and garlic; cook and stir until onion is tender. Add zucchini, broccoli and bell pepper; cook and stir until vegetables are crisp-tender, about 5 minutes.

Add chicken; stir until heated through. Stir in Italian salad dressing. Season with salt and pepper.

Add cooked pasta to skillet; mix well. Serve warm, topped with Parmesan cheese. Refrigerate leftovers.

Makes 6 servings.

Variation: Use whole wheat pasta.

One serving contains approximately: Calories 412, Fat 12g, Carbohydrates 52g, Protein 32g

Chicken Zucchini Bake

Serve with a mixed lettuce salad and buttered rolls.

1 cup dry bread crumbs
2 eggs
2 tablespoons cold water
¼ teaspoon salt
¼ teaspoon ground black pepper
2 zucchini squash, cut diagonally
   into ½-inch-thick slices
¼ cup extra virgin olive oil, divided

4 boneless, skinless chicken
   breast halves
1 pound fresh tomatoes, cored
   and thinly sliced
2 tablespoons thinly sliced fresh
   basil leaves
1¼ cups shredded mozzarella
   cheese, divided

Preheat oven to 375°. Grease a 13x9-inch baking dish.

Place bread crumbs in a shallow dish. Beat eggs, water, salt and pepper in a shallow bowl. Dip squash slices in egg mixture, then in bread crumbs, turning to coat well. Heat 1 tablespoon olive oil in a large nonstick skillet over medium heat. Add half of the breaded squash and cook 2 minutes per side; place in prepared baking dish. Repeat with 1 tablespoon olive oil and remaining squash; set aside.

Dip chicken in egg mixture, then in bread crumbs, turning to coat well. Heat remaining olive oil in same skillet; add chicken and cook 3 minutes per side or until golden brown.

Layer tomatoes and basil over squash in baking dish. Sprinkle with ¾ cup cheese. Top with chicken. Cover with baking foil. Bake in preheated oven 20 minutes. Remove from oven. Increase temperature to 400°. Uncover baking dish and sprinkle top with remaining cheese. Return to oven uncovered and bake until chicken is cooked through, about 15 minutes. Serve hot. Refrigerate leftovers.

Makes 4 servings.

One serving contains approximately: Calories 480, Fat 26g, Carbohydrates 22g, Protein 20g

Chicken Zucchini Lasagna

Serve with a lettuce salad and warm garlic bread.

10 uncooked lasagna noodles (8 ounces)
1 tablespoon butter
1 cup chopped yellow onion
2 cups sliced fresh mushrooms
2 cups ¼-inch-sliced fresh zucchini, halved
2 cups cubed cooked rotisserie chicken breast
⅓ cup water
1 14.5-ounce can diced tomatoes with
   basil, garlic and oregano
1 6-ounce can tomato paste
2 teaspoons Italian seasoning
¼ teaspoon each: salt, pepper, garlic powder

2 cups crumbled feta cheese
1 egg, slightly beaten
¼ cup chopped fresh
   flat leaf parsley
2 cups shredded mozzarella
   cheese, divided

Preheat oven to 350°. Grease 13x9-inch baking dish.
Cook lasagna following package directions; drain. Melt butter in a 12-inch nonstick skillet over medium heat. Add onion, mushrooms and zucchini; cook and stir about 7 minutes or until vegetables are crisp-tender. Stir in chicken, water, tomatoes, tomato paste, Italian seasoning, salt, pepper and garlic powder.

Mix feta cheese, egg and flat leaf parsley in a small bowl. Arrange half the cooked noodles in the prepared baking dish. Spread with half the feta cheese mixture. Spread half the sauce mixture on top of the cheese layer. Sprinkle with 1 cup mozzarella cheese. Repeat layering with remaining noodles, feta cheese mixture and sauce mixture. Cover with aluminum foil. Bake 50 minutes. Uncover; sprinkle with 1 cup mozzarella cheese and bake until melted. Remove from oven. Let stand a few minutes before serving. Serve warm. Refrigerate leftovers.

Makes 2 servings.

One serving contains approximately: Calories 250, Fat 11g, Carbohydrates 22g, Protein 19g

Goldbar Squash Rice Casserole

Serve this casserole with a green salad with Italian salad dressing.

1½ cups uncooked long grain brown rice

3 cups low-sodium chicken broth, heated until hot in a medium saucepan

4 cups diced yellow goldbar squash, or zucchini

2 medium-size green bell peppers, chopped

1 cup chopped yellow onion

¾ teaspoon salt

1½ cups milk

3 tablespoons all-purpose flour

2 cups shredded pepper Jack cheese, divided

1 cup fresh or frozen corn kernels

2 teaspoons extra virgin olive oil

½ pound turkey sausage, casings removed

4 ounces reduced fat (Neufchatel) cream cheese, cut into small pieces

¼ cup chopped pickled jalapenos

Preheat oven to 375°.
Place rice in a 13x9-inch baking dish. Stir in hot broth, goldbar squash, bell pepper, onion and salt. Cover with aluminum foil; bake 45 minutes. Remove foil and continue baking until most of the liquid is absorbed, about 40 minutes.

Whisk milk and flour in a small saucepan; cook and stir over medium heat until thickened. Stir in 1½ cups Jack cheese and corn until cheese melts; set aside.

Heat olive oil in a large skillet over medium heat. Add turkey sausage. Cook until crumbly and no longer pink, about 6 minutes; set aside.

When rice is done, stir in cheese sauce and cooked sausage. Sprinkle with ½ cup Jack cheese, cream cheese pieces and jalapenos. Return to oven; bake until cheese is melted, about 10 minutes. Let stand a few minutes before serving. Refrigerate leftovers.

Makes 12 servings.

One serving contains approximately: Calories 250, Fat 9g, Carbohydrates 29g, Protein 12g

Grilled Zucchini Quesadillas

Serve with sour cream and salsa as desired.

2 tablespoons extra virgin olive oil
1 tablespoon pureed chipotle peppers in adobo sauce, or to taste

2 small zucchini, quartered lengthwise
1 red bell pepper, seeded and cut in half lengthwise
8 whole green onions, seeded and cut in half lengthwise

2 cups shredded Mexican cheese blend, divided
8 6-inch whole wheat tortillas
¼ cup chopped fresh cilantro

Mix olive oil and pureed peppers in a small bowl; reserve 1 tablespoon of mixture. Brush remaining mixture on both sides of vegetables. Grill over medium coals about 10 minutes or until tender, turning occasionally. Cut zucchini and bell pepper crosswise into ¼-inch slices.

Sprinkle half of cheese equally over four tortillas; drizzle reserved oil mixture over cheese. Top each equally with grilled vegetables, cilantro, remaining cheese and remaining tortillas. Grill quesadillas over medium-low heat 3 minutes per side. Cut into wedges. Serve warm. Refrigerate leftovers.

Makes 4 servings.

One serving contains approximately: Calories 540, Fat 32g, Carbohydrates 45g, Protein 19g

Moose's Cheese Ravioli with Zucchini and Beef Skillet

Serve this quick meal with green salad and crusty rolls . . . buttered of course.

1 9-ounce package refrigerated fresh cheese ravioli

2 teaspoons cooking oil
1 pound lean ground beef
½ cup chopped yellow onion
2 large cloves fresh garlic, finely chopped

1 14.5-ounce can diced tomatoes
2 cups ½-inch cubed fresh zucchini
1 teaspoon dried oregano leaves
¼ teaspoon dried basil leaves
½ teaspoon salt
¼ teaspoon ground black pepper

1 cup shredded mozzarella cheese

Cook ravioli following package directions; rinse, drain and set aside.

Heat cooking oil in a 10-inch nonstick skillet over medium-high heat. Add ground beef, onion and garlic; stir and cook until beef is completely browned. Drain and discard fat.

Stir in cooked ravioli, tomatoes, zucchini, oregano, basil, salt and pepper. Cook, stirring occasionally, until zucchini is crisp-tender, about 5 minutes. Stir in cheese until melted. Serve warm. Refrigerate leftovers.

Makes 6 servings.

One serving contains approximately: Calories 330, Fat 15g, Carbohydrates 22g, Protein 26g

Open-face Turkey Burgers

Zucchini is found in this tasty burger.

1 pound ground turkey meat
1 medium-size fresh zucchini, grated
1 medium-size fresh carrot, peeled and grated
3 cloves fresh garlic, minced
½ teaspoon salt
¼ teaspoon ground black pepper
¼ teaspoon dried thyme leaves
¼ teaspoon dried oregano leaves
1 egg
1 tablespoon extra virgin olive oil

4 slices crusty bread
2 tablespoons extra virgin olive oil, mixed in a bowl with
  ¼ teaspoon garlic powder

4 tablespoons mayonnaise
4 lettuce leaves
4 slices fresh ripe tomato

Mix first 9 ingredients in a large bowl; form 4 equal-size patties. Heat 1 tablespoon olive oil in a large nonstick skillet over medium-high heat. Add patties; cook, turning once, until no pink remains, about 5 minutes each side.

Brush bread equally with olive oil mixture. Place on a baking sheet. Broil until golden. Remove from oven. Place bread on four individual plates; spread equally with mayonnaise. Add lettuce, tomato and warm turkey patty. Serve. Refrigerate leftovers.

Makes 4 servings.

One serving contains approximately: Calories 300 Fat 14g Carbohydrates 23g Protein 26g

Pork Tenderloin with Spaghetti Squash

Fennel seasoning adds a special flavor. Serve with a salad and rolls.

1 medium-size spaghetti squash,
    about 4 pounds

2 pounds pork tenderloin
¼ cup fennel seeds, crushed
2 tablespoons Italian seasoning
¾ teaspoon salt
½ teaspoon ground black pepper

3 tablespoons butter, divided
1 medium-size yellow onion,
    coarsely chopped
¾ cup purchased marinara sauce
½ cup shredded Parmesan cheese
¼ cup snipped fresh basil leaves

Cut squash in half lengthwise. Scrape and discards seeds. Place squash halves cut-side down in a 13x9-inch baking dish. Cover with microwave-safe plastic wrap. Microwave on high 10–12 minutes or until squash is very soft when pierced with a sharp knife. Set squash aside until cool enough to handle.

Preheat oven to 375°.
Rinse pork tenderloin with cold water; shake off excess water. Mix fennel, Italian seasoning, salt and pepper in a small container; press mixture onto all sides of pork. Melt 2 tablespoons butter in a large nonstick skillet. Add pork; cook over medium heat until browned on all sides. Place in a lightly greased shallow baking dish. Cook about 30 minutes or until interior of meat reaches 145°.

Melt remaining butter in same skillet. Add onion; stir and cook until soft. Scrape cooked spaghetti squash pulp (strands) into skillet. Stir in marinara sauce; cook until thoroughly heated. Stir in cheese and basil; transfer to a serving platter. Slice pork into ¼-inch-thick pieces and place over squash mixture on platter. Drizzle any juices from cooked pork on top. Serve. Refrigerate leftovers.

Makes 6 servings.

One serving contains approximately: Calories 440, Fat 20g, Carbohydrates 15g, Protein 51g

Pumpkin Pancakes

Serve with softened butter and maple syrup, along with sausage or crisp bacon.

1½ cups buttermilk
1 cup canned pumpkin puree (not pie mix)
1 egg
2 tablespoons cooking oil

2 cups all-purpose flour
½ teaspoon salt
3 tablespoons brown sugar
2 teaspoons baking powder
1 teaspoon baking soda
1 teaspoon ground cinnamon
½ teaspoon ground ginger
¼ teaspoon ground cloves

Preheat a lightly oiled pancake griddle or skillet over medium-high heat.

Mix buttermilk, pumpkin, egg and cooking oil in a large bowl.

Mix remaining ingredients in medium bowl. Stir into pumpkin mixture just until combined; do not overmix.

Pour ¼ cup batter for each pancake onto griddle or skillet; cook until brown on both sides. Serve warm. Refrigerate leftovers.

Makes 6 servings.

One serving contains approximately: Calories 278, Fat 8g, Carbohydrates 46g, Protein 7g

Pumpkin Waffles

Serve these delicious waffles with warm maple syrup or syrup of your choice.

1 cup plus 2 tablespoons all-purpose flour
½ teaspoon salt
½ teaspoon baking powder
¼ teaspoon baking soda
1 teaspoon ground cinnamon
⅛ teaspoon ground nutmeg
2 tablespoons packed brown sugar

2 eggs beaten
2T butter or margarine, melted + cooled

1 cup whole milk
½ cup canned pumpkin

½ cup softened butter mixed in a small bowl
   with ¼ cup toasted chopped pecans and
   1 tablespoon orange marmalade

Preheat waffle iron.

Mix flour, salt, baking powder, soda, cinnamon, nutmeg and sugar in a large bowl.
eggs + melted/cooled butter
Mix milk and pumpkin in a small bowl. Add to flour mixture, and stir until just
combined; do not overmix.

Cook in a preheated waffle iron, following manufacturer's directions, until
golden brown. Top each serving (2 waffles) with 2 tablespoons butter mixture.
Serve warm. Refrigerate leftovers.

Makes 4 servings.

One serving contains approximately: Calories 540, Fat 38g, Carbohydrates 41g, Protein 11g

Quick Chicken Cacciatore

Serve over angel hair pasta or white rice.

¼ cup all-purpose flour
2 pounds boneless, skinless chicken thighs, lightly seasoned
with salt and ground black pepper

1 tablespoon butter
1 tablespoon cooking oil
¼ cup finely chopped yellow onion
2 large cloves fresh garlic, finely chopped

1 14-ounce jar spaghetti sauce
½ cup low-sodium chicken broth
1 cup sliced baby zucchini

Place flour in a large food-grade plastic bag. Add chicken; shake to coat well.

Heat butter and cooking oil in a 10-inch nonstick skillet until hot. Add chicken, onion and garlic; cook over medium heat, turning occasionally, until chicken is lightly browned. Drain and discard fat.

Mix spaghetti sauce and chicken broth in a medium container; pour over chicken in skillet and continue cooking over medium heat until mixture comes to a full boil. Reduce heat to low. Add zucchini. Cover and cook until chicken is tender, about 30 minutes. Serve. Refrigerate leftovers.

Makes 6 servings.

One serving contains approximately: Calories 350, Fat 18g, Carbohydrates 10g, Protein 29g

Ramen-Zucchini-Chicken Skillet

The college kids will love this quick meal!

1½ cups water
2 3-ounce packages chicken flavored Ramen noodle soup
1 small yellow onion, chopped

1 medium fresh zucchini, diced
1 fresh tomato, diced
2 cups diced cooked rotisserie chicken meat

Bring water to a boil in a large skillet over medium heat. Stir in contents of soup seasoning packets. Add onion; cover and cook until onion is soft, about 5 minutes.

Break noodles into pieces and add to skillet.

Add zucchini, tomato and chicken; cover and continue cooking until noodles are tender, about 10 minutes. Serve. Refrigerate leftovers.

Makes 4 servings.

One serving contains approximately: Calories 260, Fat 16g, Carbohydrates 7g, Protein 20g

Ruth's Fish with Summer Squash

My sister, Ruth, serves this dish over hot white rice, along with a green salad.

1 tablespoon extra virgin olive oil
1 red onion, chopped
2 small yellow summer squash, cut into ½-inch pieces
2 large cloves fresh garlic, finely chopped
1 fresh jalapeno, seeded and thinly sliced, or to taste
½ teaspoon salt
¼ teaspoon freshly ground black pepper
1 28-ounce can diced tomatoes, undrained

4 6-ounce pieces skinless halibut filet, or other firm fish

Heat olive oil in a large skillet over medium heat. Add onion; stir and cook until soft, about 6 minutes. Add squash, garlic, jalapeno, ½ teaspoon salt and ¼ teaspoon black pepper. Cook, stirring occasionally, until squash begins to soften, about 4 minutes. Stir in tomatoes.

Season halibut with salt and pepper to taste; add to skillet and cover with vegetable mixture. Cover skillet and simmer over medium-low heat until halibut is opaque throughout and beginning to flake, about 10–12 minutes. Serve warm. Refrigerate leftovers.

Makes 4 servings.

One serving contains approximately: Calories 297, Fat 8g, Carbohydrates 13g, Protein 41g

Salmon and Squash Skillet

Serve plain or over hot couscous or angel hair pasta.

1 tablespoon butter
1 tablespoon cooking oil
1 pound skinless 1-inch-thick salmon fillets

2 small zucchinis cut into ½-inch pieces
1 cup ½-inch pieces yellow summer squash
½ teaspoon salt
¼ teaspoon ground black pepper
½ cup halved cherry tomatoes
2 tablespoons chopped fresh basil leaves

Heat butter and oil in a 12-inch nonstick skillet over medium heat. Add salmon; cook, turning once, until lightly browned, about 5 minutes.

Add zucchini, yellow squash, salt and pepper. Cover and cook until squash is crisp-tender and salmon flakes, about 5 minutes. Add tomatoes; cook 3 minutes. Remove from heat; sprinkle with basil. Serve. Refrigerate leftovers.

Makes 6 servings.

One serving contains approximately: Calories 280 Fat, 15g, Carbohydrates 4g, Protein 30

Salmon Kabobs

Serve with rice pilaf and crisp green salad.

1 pound fresh salmon, cut into 1-inch cubes
4 cups total: zucchini, bell pepper and red onion cubes
Salt and black pepper to taste

3 tablespoons minced shallots
1½ tablespoons basil olive oil
1½ tablespoons pesto
1½ tablespoons white balsamic vinegar

Thread salmon and vegetables onto skewers; season with salt and black pepper.
Place on a well-oiled grill over medium heat. Cook 10–15 minutes, turning once or
twice, until salmon is cooked through to an internal temperature of 150°. Place on
a platter.

Mix shallots, olive oil, pesto and vinegar in a small bowl; pour over cooked kabobs.
Serve warm. Refrigerate leftovers.

Makes 4 servings.

One serving contains approximately: Calories 310, Fat 16g, Carbohydrates 11g, Protein 28g

Sam's Stuffed Zucchini

Serve with a lettuce and tomato salad and crusty rolls . . . like Sam, unforgettable.

4 8-inch garden fresh zucchinis

1 pound sweet Italian sausage links,
  casings removed

2 tablespoons extra virgin olive
  oil, divided
½ cup finely chopped yellow onion
2 cloves fresh garlic, finely chopped

½ cup unsweetened apple juice
½ teaspoon salt
¼ teaspoon ground black pepper
½ cup Italian seasoned dried
  bread crumbs
1 cup shredded mozzarella
  with sun-dried tomatoes and
  basil, divided
1 egg, lightly beaten

Preheat oven to 350°. Grease a 13x9-inch baking dish.

Cut zucchinis in half lengthwise, then in half crosswise. Remove pulp with a small knife, leaving a ¼-inch shell. Chop pulp and set aside. Cook zucchini shells in boiling salted water just until crisp-tender, about 2 minutes. Remove from pot and place in a single layer in prepared baking dish. Sprinkle with salt and pepper.

Stir and cook sausage in a large nonstick skillet over medium heat until crumbly and no longer pink. Drain well; set aside. Heat 1 tablespoon olive oil in same skillet. Add chopped onion; cook and stir over medium heat 2 minutes. Stir in chopped pulp and garlic; cook and stir until vegetables are crisp-tender, about 2 minutes. Stir in apple juice; cook until juice is reduced by half. Stir in salt, pepper, drained sausage, bread crumbs, ½ cup cheese and egg. Spoon mixture equally into zucchini shells. Drizzle 1 tablespoon olive oil over all. Top with remaining cheese.

Bake about 15 minutes or until cheese has melted. If desired, broil until lightly browned. Serve warm. Refrigerate leftovers.

Makes 4 servings.

One serving contains approximately: Calories 416, Fat 24g, Carbohydrates 17g, Protein 29g

Sausage and Zucchini Pizza

Serve with a mixed green salad tossed with Italian salad dressing.

4 tablespoons extra virgin olive oil, divided
12 ounces sweet Italian sausage links, sliced

2 10-ounce portions frozen pizza dough, thawed
2 medium-size zucchini, thinly sliced
1½ cups roasted red peppers, drained and thinly sliced
1 teaspoon dried thyme
½ teaspoon dried oregano leaves
½ teaspoon salt
¼ teaspoon ground black pepper

1 cup grated provolone cheese, or other cheese

Preheat oven to 475°.

Heat 2 tablespoons olive oil in a large nonstick skillet over medium-high heat. Add sausage; brown on both sides until almost cooked, about 3 minutes. Drain on paper towels; set aside.

Roll out dough on a floured surface into two 10x14-inch rectangles; place on ungreased baking sheets. Top dough with drained sausage, zucchini and peppers. Sprinkle with thyme and oregano. Drizzle with remaining olive oil, and sprinkle evenly with salt and pepper. Bake 15 minutes.

Remove from oven. Top with cheese. Return to oven; bake until sausage is cooked and the cheese melts. Remove from oven. Cut and serve. Refrigerate leftovers.

Makes 4 servings.

One serving contains approximately: Calories 699, Fat 35g, Carbohydrates 71g, Protein 33g

Saucy Zucchini Pasta Skillet

A mixed lettuce salad, dressed with Italian salad dressing, will complement this tasty meal. Serve with warm French bread or rolls.

8 ounces dried uncooked
  penne pasta

3 tablespoons butter
1 medium-size yellow onion, cut
  into 1-inch pieces
3 large cloves fresh garlic

4 cups ½-inch slices fresh zucchini
1 red bell pepper, seeded and
  thinly sliced
1 yellow or green bell pepper,
  seeded and thinly sliced

1 teaspoon salt
½ teaspoon coarsely ground
  black pepper

2 large ripe tomatoes cut into
  ½-inch pieces
¾ cup freshly grated Parmesan cheese
2 tablespoons chopped fresh basil or
  2 teaspoons dried basil leaves
¼ teaspoon dried oregano leaves

5 deli-style provolone cheese slices, cut
  into thin strips then coarsely chopped

Cook pasta following package directions; drain and set aside.

Melt butter in a large nonstick skillet. Stir in onion; cook and stir over medium-high heat until lightly browned. Add garlic; stir and cook 2 minutes. Add zucchini, bell peppers, salt and pepper. Stir and cook until vegetables are crisp-tender.

Stir in cooked pasta, tomatoes, Parmesan cheese, basil and oregano; cook and stir until thoroughly heated.

Sprinkle top with provolone cheese; cover and let stand until melted. Serve warm. Refrigerate leftovers.

Makes 8 servings.

One serving contains approximately: Calories 330, Fat 14g, Carbohydrates 39g, Protein 16g

Savory Zucchini Pie

Serve this savory pie for a light lunch along with a garden salad.

3 cups grated unpeeled firm zucchini
½ cup chopped yellow onion
1 large clove fresh garlic, finely chopped
1 cup all-purpose flour
1 cup grated provolone cheese
4 tablespoons grated Parmesan cheese, divided
3 eggs, beaten
¼ cup cooking oil
2 teaspoons chopped fresh basil
1 teaspoon baking powder
½ teaspoon salt
½ teaspoon ground black pepper

Preheat oven to 350°. Grease a 10-inch glass pie plate.

Mix all ingredients except 1 tablespoon Parmesan cheese in a large bowl. Spoon mixture into prepared pie plate. Bake until golden brown, about 45–50 minutes.

Remove from oven; sprinkle with 1 tablespoon Parmesan cheese. Cool slightly before serving. Refrigerate leftovers.

Makes 6 servings.

Variation: Add fresh chopped parsley and dill instead of basil.

One serving contains approximately: Calories 289, Fat 18g, Carbohydrates 20g, Protein 12g

Shrimp and Zucchini Skillet

This tasty dish is ready to enjoy in minutes. Serve with warm crusty bread, or over hot white rice or angel hair pasta.

¼ cup extra virgin olive oil
6 large cloves fresh garlic, finely chopped
3 tablespoons fresh oregano, finely chopped

2 pounds raw medium-size shrimp, peeled and deveined
¾ pound fresh zucchini, cut into ½-inch cubes
1 cup red cherry tomatoes, halved
½ cup yellow cherry tomatoes, halved
½ cup fresh basil, chopped
¼ teaspoon salt
⅛ teaspoon ground black pepper

Fresh lemon, sliced for garnish, optional

Heat olive oil in a large nonstick skillet over high heat. Add garlic and oregano; stir and cook 30 seconds.

Add shrimp and zucchini; stir and cook about 5 minutes or until shrimp are opaque in center. Stir in tomatoes, basil, salt and pepper; cook 2 minutes.

Serve immediately. Garnish with lemon slices, if desired. Refrigerate leftovers.

Makes 6 servings.

One serving contains approximately: Calories 220, Fat 11g, Carbohydrates 6g, Protein 26g

Soft Veggie Tacos

Serve warm with favorite beverage.

1 tablespoon cooking oil
1 medium onion, chopped
1 cup diced zucchini
1 cup diced crookneck yellow squash
3 cloves garlic, minced
1 jalapeno, seeded and chopped (or to taste)
4 medium tomatoes, seeded and chopped
1 cup fresh corn kernels (or frozen)
½ cup fresh cilantro, chopped
1 cup canned pinto beans or black beans, rinsed

8 corn tortillas

Heat oil in a large skillet; add onion and cook until tender. Add zucchini and yellow squash; stir and continue cooking for about 5 minutes. Add garlic, jalapeno and half of the tomatoes. Reduce heat to medium-low and cook until flavors combine, about 10 minutes.

Add corn kernels; stir and cook until kernels are tender crisp. Stir in the cilantro, the remaining tomatoes and beans; remove from heat.

Warm the tortillas on a hot, dry skillet. Fill each with the vegetable mixture. Top with salsa and serve. Refrigerate leftovers.

Makes 4 servings.

Variation: Use flour tortillas instead of corn tortillas.

One serving contains approximately: Calories 300, Fat 6g, Carbohydrates 56g, Protein 10g

Spaghetti and Zucchini Pancakes

Serve these savory pancakes for a light lunch, along with a lettuce and tomato salad.

8-ounces dried uncooked spaghetti

5 tablespoons extra virgin olive oil, divided
1 medium-size yellow onion, chopped
1 medium zucchini, grated

2 eggs, beaten
¾ cup grated Pecorino Romano cheese (3 ounces)
½ teaspoon salt
¼ teaspoon freshly ground black pepper

1 cup purchased marinara sauce

Cook spaghetti following package directions; drain and place in a large bowl.

Heat 1 tablespoon olive oil in a large nonstick skillet over medium-high heat. Add onion and zucchini; cook and stir until soft, about 8 minutes. Add to bowl with cooked spaghetti. Add eggs, cheese, salt and pepper; mix well.

Heat remaining 4 tablespoons olive oil in a large nonstick skillet over medium heat. Working in batches, cook ½-cup portions of mixture until golden and crisp, about 4 minutes per side. Serve warm with marinara sauce. Refrigerate leftovers.

Makes 4 servings.

One serving contains approximately: Calories 548, Fat 28g, Carbohydrates 54g, Protein 18g

Spaghetti Squash with Pancetta

Serve with a crisp green salad, along with hard rolls . . . buttered of course.

2½-pound spaghetti squash

6 strips pancetta, coarsely chopped
2 large fresh tomatoes, seeded and chopped
1 teaspoon garlic salt
¼ teaspoon ground black pepper
⅓ cup shredded Parmesan cheese
¼ cup chopped toasted walnuts
3 tablespoons snipped fresh basil

Cut squash in half lengthwise; scoop out seeds with a spoon and discard. Place squash in a shallow microwave-safe dish with ½ inch water. Cover with plastic wrap and cook on high 10 minutes, or until tender. Cool slightly. Scrape pulp with a fork into strands; set aside.

Cook pancetta in a large nonstick skillet over medium-high heat until crisp. Remove from skillet; set aside. Add tomatoes to skillet; cook and stir 2 minutes. Add cooked squash, garlic salt and pepper to skillet; cook and stir until very hot, about 5 minutes. Add cooked pancetta, cheese, walnuts and basil; toss lightly. Serve. Refrigerate leftovers.

Makes 6 servings.

Variation: Use thick-cut bacon instead of pancetta.

One serving contains approximately: Calories 170, Fat 10g, Carbohydrates 16g, Protein 5g

Spicy Shrimp and Zucchini

A green salad will complete this tasty meal.

1 pound raw medium-size shrimp

1 tablespoon butter
1 tablespoon cooking oil
3 cups ½-inch sliced fresh zucchini
½ cup finely chopped yellow onion
2 large cloves finely chopped fresh garlic
1 14-ounce can diced tomatoes with Italian herbs
½ teaspoon salt or to taste
¼ teaspoon ground red pepper or ground black pepper

4 cups hot cooked white rice

Bring water to a boil in a medium saucepan; add shrimp and boil until cooked, about 3 minutes. Remove shrimp and set aside.

Heat butter and cooking oil in a 10-inch nonstick skillet over medium-high heat. Add zucchini, onion and garlic; stir and cook 3 minutes. Stir in tomatoes, salt and pepper. Cook until mixture comes to a full boil, about 3 minutes. Reduce heat to medium. Cover and cook, stirring occasionally, 10 minutes.

Serve hot over rice. Refrigerate leftovers.

Makes 6 servings.

One serving contains approximately: Calories 390, Fat 7g, Carbohydrates 53g, Protein 24g

Stuffed Turban Squash

Serve as a side dish, or serve as a light lunch, along with a garden salad and rolls.

1 3-pound turban squash

2 tablespoons butter
¼ cup chopped yellow onion
1 rib celery, chopped
1 fresh carrot, finely diced
½ pound pork sausage

¼ cup soft bread crumbs
2 tablespoons light brown sugar
1 teaspoon salt
½ teaspoon black pepper

Preheat oven to 350°. Grease a baking sheet.

Cut top off turban squash; set top aside. Scoop out seeds; discard. Place squash cut-side down on prepared baking sheet. Cover with baking foil. Bake until tender, about 50–60 minutes. Remove from oven. Scoop pulp from cavity; set aside.

Heat butter in a nonstick saucepan. Add onion, celery, carrot and sausage; cook and stir over medium heat until vegetables are tender; drain and discard fat.

Stir in bread crumbs, sugar, salt, pepper and cooked squash pulp. Spoon filling into cavity of squash. Cover with the top that was set aside. Bake until heated through, about 25 minutes. Serve hot. Refrigerate leftovers.

Makes 4 servings.

One serving contains approximately: Calories 262, Fat 21g, Carbohydrates 9g, Protein 8g

Tuna-Zucchini Patties

For a quick and tasty lunch, serve on a warm bun, topped with a slice of tomato and pickles, along with a side of potato chips.

2 tablespoons margarine
1 cup finely chopped yellow onion

2 6.5-ounce cans light water-packed tuna, well drained
2 cups shredded fresh zucchini
4 eggs, lightly beaten in a small bowl
⅔ cup finely chopped flat leaf parsley
2 teaspoons fresh lemon juice
1 teaspoon salt
½ teaspoon ground black pepper
2 cups seasoned bread crumbs, divided

¼ cup cooking oil, divided

Heat margarine in a large nonstick saucepan over medium heat. Add chopped onion; cook and stir until tender. Add tuna, zucchini, eggs, parsley, lemon juice, salt, black pepper and 1 cup bread crumbs; stir together until combined. Shape mixture into twelve ½-inch-thick patties; coat with remaining bread crumbs.

Heat 2 tablespoons cooking oil in a large nonstick skillet over medium heat. Cook 6 patties at a time, 3 minutes on each side, or until golden brown. Remove and set aside. Heat remaining cooking oil in same skillet; cook remaining 6 patties. Serve warm. Refrigerate leftovers.

Makes 6 servings.

One serving contains approximately: Calories 400, Fat 19g, Carbohydrates 31g, Protein 26g

Turkey Pumpkin Chili

Serve this tasty chili plain in bowls along with crisp crackers, or serve over hot white rice along with a green salad dressed with Italian salad dressing.

2 tablespoons cooking oil
1 medium-size yellow onion, chopped
1 small green bell pepper, chopped
3 cloves fresh garlic, finely chopped
1 jalapeno pepper, finely chopped, seeds discarded

1 pound ground turkey meat
1 14-ounce can diced tomatoes
1 15-ounce can pumpkin puree (not pie mix)
1 cup water
1 tablespoon chili powder
1 teaspoon ground cumin
½ teaspoon dried oregano leaves
¼ teaspoon ground black pepper
Salt to taste
1 15-ounce can kidney beans, drained

Heat oil in a large saucepan over medium-high heat. Add onion, bell pepper and garlic; stir and cook until soft, about 4 minutes. Stir in chopped jalapeno.

Add turkey to saucepan; stir and cook until browned. Add tomatoes, pumpkin puree, water, chili powder, cumin, oregano, black pepper and salt. Bring mixture to a boil. Stir in beans. Reduce heat, cover and simmer, stirring occasionally, for 30 minutes. Serve hot. Refrigerate leftovers.

Makes 6 servings.

One serving contains approximately: Calories 290, Fat 3g, Carbohydrates 23g Protein 20g

Two-Squash Enchiladas

Zucchini and yellow squash are used in this recipe. Serve with sour cream and sliced green onion, as desired.

1 medium-size yellow onion, chopped
¾ cup diced zucchini
¾ cup yellow squash
¾ cup diced fresh tomatoes
½ cup corn kernels
1 4-ounce can diced green chilies
1 2.25-ounce can sliced ripe olives, drained
2 teaspoons Mexican seasoning

2 14-ounce cans red or green enchilada sauce
1 14-ounce package corn tortillas
1 8-ounce package shredded reduced-fat Mexican cheese, divided

Preheat oven to 375°. Lightly grease bottom of a 13x9-inch baking dish.

Spray a large nonstick skillet with cooking spray; heat over medium heat. Add onion; cook and stir 10 minutes. Add zucchini, yellow squash, tomatoes, corn, chilies, olives and seasoning; cook and stir 5 minutes.

Cover bottom of prepared baking dish with enchilada sauce. Place tortillas on a microwave-safe plate. Cover with damp paper towel. Microwave on high 1 minute to soften. Dip each tortilla in enchilada sauce; spoon about ⅓ cup vegetables and 1 tablespoon cheese onto each. Roll up and place seam-side down in baking dish.

Cover loosely with aluminum foil. Bake 30 minutes. Remove foil and sprinkle with remaining cheese and continue baking, 10 minutes. Serve. Refrigerate leftovers.

Makes 10 servings.

One serving contains approximately: Calories 240, Fat 12g, Carbohydrates 27g, Protein 11g

Vegetable Soft Tacos

Serve this quick meal with mint iced tea.

1 tablespoon cooking oil
1 large yellow onion, quartered and sliced
1 cup ¼-inch cubed butternut squash
1 cup diced red bell pepper
1 8-ounce package sliced mushrooms
1 8-ounce pouch taco sauce

8 small corn or flour tortillas, warmed
1 cup shredded Monterey Jack cheese
Torn fresh cilantro leaves

Heat cooking oil in a large skillet over medium-high heat. Add vegetables; cook and stir 10 minutes. Stir in sauce; cover and cook 5 minutes.

Spoon mixture into tortillas and top with cheese and cilantro. Serve. Refrigerate leftovers.

Makes 4 servings.

One serving contains approximately: Calories 320, Fat 14g, Carbohydrates 38g, Protein 10g

Zucchini Alfredo

Serve with a green salad and warm French bread.

2½ pounds fresh zucchini (about 5)
1 teaspoon salt

2 tablespoons extra virgin olive oil
3 cloves fresh garlic, minced

1 8-ounce package cream cheese, cubed and softened
¾ cups half-and-half or light cream
½ cup finely shredded Parmesan cheese
Coarsely ground black pepper
Ground nutmeg
Finely shredded Parmesan cheese

Cut zucchini in half crosswise. Then cut lengthwise into ¼-inch-thick slices, and then lengthwise into long thin strips about ¼-inch wide (fettuccine-like strips). You should have about 8 cups. Toss zucchini strips with salt in a colander; let drain 1 hour, then rinse and drain well. Pat dry.

Heat olive oil in a 12-inch nonstick skillet over medium-high heat. Add zucchini and garlic; cook and stir until crisp-tender, about 4 minutes; place in a large bowl.

In the same skillet, over medium-low heat, stir and heat cream cheese and half-and-half until smooth. Stir in ½ cup Parmesan cheese. Stir in zucchini; heat through. Transfer to a large serving dish. Sprinkle with pepper, nutmeg and additional Parmesan cheese as desired. Serve. Refrigerate leftovers.

Makes 8 servings.

One serving contains approximately: Calories 351, Fat 27g, Carbohydrates 7g, Protein 20g

Zucchini Beef Ravioli Skillet

Serve with a green salad and warm Italian bread.

1 9-ounce package refrigerated cheese ravioli

1 tablespoon extra virgin olive oil
1 pound lean ground beef
½ teaspoon salt
¼ teaspoon ground black pepper
½ cup chopped yellow onion
2 cloves fresh garlic, minced

1 14-ounce can diced tomatoes
2 cups ½-inch cubed fresh zucchini
1 teaspoon dried oregano leaves
½ teaspoon dried basil leaves

1 cup shredded mozzarella cheese

Cook ravioli following package directions; drain and rinse.

Heat olive oil in a 10-inch nonstick skillet over medium-high heat. Add ground beef, salt, black pepper, onion and garlic; stir and cook until beef is browned, about 7 minutes. Drain fat.

Stir in tomatoes, zucchini, oregano, basil and cooked ravioli. Cook, stirring occasionally, until zucchini is tender, about 5 minutes. Stir in cheese until melted. Serve warm. Refrigerate leftovers.

Makes 6 servings.

One serving contains approximately: Calories 340, Fat 15g, Carbohydrates 22g, Protein 25g

Zucchini Frittata

Serve this egg dish for a special breakfast along with assorted muffins or toast.

6 eggs, slightly beaten
¼ cup milk
1 medium-size yellow onion, chopped
½ teaspoon dried basil
¼ teaspoon salt
¼ teaspoon ground black pepper

3 tablespoons butter
2 cloves fresh garlic, finely chopped

1 medium-size zucchini, sliced
  diagonally into ¼-inch slices
1 fresh ripe tomato, cut into
  6 slices
½ cup shredded mozzarella cheese
3 tablespoons freshly grated
  Parmesan cheese

Preheat oven to 350°.

Mix eggs, milk, onion, basil, salt and pepper in a medium bowl; set aside.

Melt butter over high heat in a 10-inch ovenproof skillet until hot. Add garlic; stir and cook over medium heat 2 minutes, then immediately pour egg mixture into skillet.

Bake in preheated oven until egg whites are partially set, about 8–10 minutes.

Remove from oven. Place zucchini slices in a circle on top of egg mixture, then place tomato slices over zucchini slices. Sprinkle with cheeses.

Return to oven and bake until egg is set and cheese is melted, about 10–14 minutes. Remove from oven; cut and serve. Refrigerate leftovers.

Makes 6 servings.

One serving contains approximately: Calories 180, Fat 14g, Carbohydrates 4g, Protein 11g

Zucchini Pizza Bake

This 3-cheese pizza bake is sure to become a favorite.

4 cups shredded unpeeled zucchini
½ teaspoon salt
2 eggs, slightly beaten
½ cup grated Parmesan cheese
2 cups shredded mozzarella
    cheese, divided
1 cup shredded Monterey Jack
    cheese, divided

1 tablespoon cooking oil
1 pound ground beef
¼ teaspoon salt, or to taste
¼ teaspoon ground black pepper
½ cup chopped yellow onion
1 15-ounce can Italian-style
    tomato sauce
1 teaspoon Italian seasoning
1 green bell pepper, chopped
½ cup sliced fresh mushrooms
½ cup sliced black olives

Preheat oven to 400°. Grease a 13x9-inch baking dish.

Place shredded zucchini in a colander; sprinkle with salt and let drain 15 minutes, then squeeze out moisture. Mix zucchini, eggs, Parmesan, 1 cup mozzarella and ½ cup Monterey Jack cheese in a large bowl. Press mixture into prepared baking dish. Bake uncovered 20 minutes. Remove from oven.

Heat cooking oil in a large nonstick skillet. Add ground beef, salt, black pepper and onion. Cook and stir until beef is crumbly and no long pink. Drain and discard fat. Stir in tomatoes and Italian seasoning. Spoon mixture over the baked zucchini crust. Top with bell pepper, mushrooms, black olives and remaining cheeses.

Return to preheated oven. Bake 20 minutes or until heated through. Remove from oven; let rest a few minutes before cutting. Serve. Refrigerate leftovers.

Makes 6 servings.

One serving contains approximately: Calories 400, Fat 25g, Carbohydrates 13g, Protein 33g

Sides

Acorn-Butternut-Fennel Casserole

Both acorn and butternut squash are featured in this delicious side dish.

4 cups ½-inch cubed peeled
    butternut squash
2 tablespoons water, divided
4 cups ½-inch cubed peeled
    acorn squash

1 tablespoon butter
2 cups coarsely chopped fennel,
    white bottom only
1 cup chopped yellow onion

1 cup diced Havarti cheese
1 8-ounce container
    mascarpone cheese
½ teaspoon salt, or to taste
¼ teaspoon ground black pepper

Preheat oven to 400°. Butter a 2-quart baking dish.

Place butternut squash and 1 tablespoon water in a large microwave-safe dish and cover tightly. Microwave on high 7 minutes or until squash is tender, stirring once; drain and place in a bowl. Repeat procedure for acorn squash with remaining 1 tablespoon water.

Melt butter in a large nonstick skillet over medium heat. Add fennel and onion; cook and stir until onion is tender, about 8 minutes. Remove skillet from heat. Stir in cheeses, microwaved squash, salt and pepper. Spoon mixture into prepared baking dish.

Bake until bubbly and lightly browned, about 20 minutes. Refrigerate leftovers.

Makes 6 to 8 servings.

One serving contains approximately: Calories 370, Fat 25g, Carbohydrates 31g, Protein 11g

Acorn Squash Bake

Feta is the star in this delicious casserole. Makes a great potluck dish.

2 large acorn squash, cut in half,
   seeded and baked until tender

2 tablespoons butter
1 tablespoon margarine
1 cup chopped yellow onion
2 cloves fresh garlic, finely chopped
½ cup chopped green bell pepper
½ cup chopped red bell pepper

2 eggs
1 8-ounce container plain yogurt
1 cup crumbled feta cheese
  (4 ounces)
1 teaspoon salt
½ teaspoon ground black pepper
¼ cup hulled pumpkin or
  sunflower seeds

Preheat oven to 375°. Grease an 11x7-inch baking dish.

Scoop flesh out of baked squash. Place in a large bowl; mash and cool slightly.

Heat butter and margarine in a large skillet over medium heat. Add onion, garlic and bell peppers; cook and stir until crisp-tender.

Beat eggs in a large bowl. Stir in yogurt until blended. Stir in feta cheese, salt, black pepper, sautéed vegetables and mashed squash. Spoon mixture into prepared baking dish. Sprinkle with seeds.

Cover and bake 25 minutes. Uncover and continue baking another 30 minutes. Remove from oven. Serve warm. Refrigerate leftovers.

Makes 6 servings.

One serving contains approximately: Calories 188, Fat 11g, Carbohydrates 15g, Protein 7g

Acorn Squash Casserole

Acorn squash makes a delicious side that's so easy to prepare.

Pecan Topping
3 tablespoons cold butter
½ cup brown sugar, packed
½ cup all-purpose flour
¼ teaspoon salt
½ cup coarsely chopped pecans

3 baked acorn squash, cooled
2 eggs
½ cup granulated sugar
½ teaspoon salt
¼ cup light cream
2 tablespoons butter
1 teaspoon pure vanilla extract

Preheat oven to 350°. Grease an 11x7-inch baking dish.

Pecan Topping: Mix all topping ingredients in a medium bowl until crumbly.

Remove pulp from cooled baked squash and place in a large bowl; beat with an electric mixer until smooth. Add eggs, granulated sugar, salt, cream, 2 tablespoons butter and vanilla extract. Beat until blended. Spoon mixture into prepared baking dish. Sprinkle evenly with pecan topping.

Bake about 45 minutes or until lightly browned. Serve warm. Refrigerate leftovers.

Makes 8 servings.

Variation: Use chopped walnuts instead of pecans.

One serving contains approximately: Calories 347, Fat 15g, Carbohydrates 51g, Protein 4g

Acorn Squash with Cranberries

Serve this delicious side with roast chicken, turkey or baked ham.

2 small acorn squash, halved lengthwise and seeded

2 tablespoons orange juice
3 tablespoons granulated sugar
1 teaspoon freshly grated orange rind
1 tablespoon butter
½ teaspoon pure vanilla extract
1 cup fresh cranberries, washed, stemmed and picked over

Preheat oven to 350°.

Place squash cut-side up in a 13x9x2-inch baking pan. Cover with aluminum foil. Bake until tender but not mushy, about 30 to 35 minutes. Remove the baking pan from oven, leaving squash in pan; remove foil.

In a small saucepan, heat and stir orange juice, sugar, orange rind and butter over medium heat until sugar is dissolved and butter melted. Add vanilla extract. Stir in cranberries until coated. Spoon some of cranberry mixture into each squash cavity.

Bake squash uncovered about 15–20 minutes or until cranberries are soft. Remove squash from pan to a serving platter. Serve warm. Refrigerate leftovers.

Makes 4 servings.

One serving contains approximately: Calories 182, Fat 3g, Carbohydrates 41g, Protein 2g

Asparagus and Butternut Squash Brown Rice Risotto

Choose young tender asparagus when making this quick risotto.

1 tablespoon butter
1½ cups ¼-inch diced butternut squash
1 cup chopped yellow onion

1 cup quick-cooking brown rice
1 teaspoon dried thyme
1 32-ounce container vegetable stock or broth, warmed

1 cup 1-inch pieces thin asparagus
½ cup shredded Parmesan cheese

Melt butter in a large skillet over medium-high heat. Add squash and onion; cook and stir 5 minutes.

Stir in rice and thyme. Stir in warm stock, ½ cup at a time. Cook, stirring frequently, until excess liquid has been cooked off before each addition of more stock.

Add asparagus halfway through cooking. When all stock has been absorbed, stir in Parmesan cheese. Serve immediately. Refrigerate leftovers.

Makes 4 servings.

One serving contains approximately: Calories 294, Fat 7g, Carbohydrates 51g, Protein 10g

Baked Acorn Squash

This is a good side to serve in place of potatoes.

1 1½-pound acorn squash
¼ teaspoon salt
⅛ teaspoon ground black pepper
1 tablespoon butter, softened
½ teaspoon olive oil
1 teaspoon chopped fresh flat leaf parsley

Preheat oven to 375°. Grease a 15x10x1-inch jelly roll pan.

Cut squash in half lengthwise; discard seeds. Sprinkle insides with salt and pepper then rub insides with butter. Places halves cut-side down on prepared baking pan. Rub tops with olive oil.

Bake until fork tender, about 45 minutes. Serve warm. Refrigerate leftovers.

Makes 4 servings.

One serving contains approximately: Calories 80, Fat 4g, Carbohydrates 14g, Protein 1g

Baked Butternut Squash with Thyme

Fresh thyme adds a special flavor to this side dish.

2 butternut squash cut in half lengthwise, seeds discarded
2 tablespoons butter
½ teaspoon salt
¼ teaspoon black pepper
Fresh thyme sprigs

Preheat oven to 350°. Grease a 15x10x1-inch jelly roll pan.

Place squash halves cut-side up on prepared baking pan. Place 1 tablespoon butter in each half. Sprinkle with salt and pepper. Top each with a sprig of fresh thyme.

Bake until tender, about 40 minutes. Remove from oven; cool slightly. To serve, slice squash or scoop out flesh from squash into a bowl. Discard thyme. Serve warm. Refrigerate leftovers.

Makes 8 servings.

One serving contains approximately: Calories 137, Fat 6g, Carbohydrates 22g, Protein 2g

Baked Spaghetti Squash

Serve plain or buttered, seasoned with salt and pepper.

1 spaghetti squash, about 3 pounds

Preheat oven to 375°.

Cut squash in half lengthwise. Use a spoon to scoop out the seeds; discard.

Place squash in a 13x9-inch baking dish, cut-side down. Pour ½ cup water into the dish. Bake until tender, about 45 minutes.

Rake a fork back and forth across cooked squash to remove the cooked strands. Serve warm. Refrigerate leftovers.

Makes 4 servings.

One serving contains approximately: Calories 70, Fat 0.5g, Carbohydrates 17g, Protein 2g

Banana Squash with Pears

Serve this sweet side with chicken, turkey or ham for a special treat.

1¼-pounds banana squash, peeled and evenly cut into
    ¼-inch slices
2 ripe but firm Bartlett pears, peeled, cored and sliced

2 tablespoons butter, melted
2 tablespoons brown sugar
2 tablespoons maple syrup
½ teaspoon allspice
⅛ teaspoon ground ginger

Place squash and pears in an 11x7-inch glass baking dish. Cover with microwave-safe plastic wrap. Microwave on high until tender, about 8 minutes. Holding hot dish with a towel or oven mitt, carefully turn back a corner of plastic wrap and drain off any liquid.

Stir together remaining ingredients in a small bowl; drizzle over squash. Let stand a few minutes before serving. Refrigerate leftovers.

Makes 8 servings.

One serving contains approximately: Calories 90, Fat 3g, Carbohydrates 16g, Protein 1g

Buttercup Squash with Apples

Delicious served with pan-fried slices of ham.

1 small buttercup squash, peeled, seeded and cut into ½-inch cubes
½ cup water

2 Golden Delicious apples, peeled, cored and cubed
2 tablespoons granulated sugar
½ teaspoon ground cinnamon
¼ teaspoon ground nutmeg
¼ teaspoon salt
1 tablespoon butter

Place squash and water in a 1½-quart microwave-safe casserole. Cover and microwave on high, stirring once during cooking, until tender, about 7 minutes.

Stir in apples, sugar, cinnamon, nutmeg, salt and butter. Cover and microwave on high until tender, stirring once during cooking. Serve warm. Refrigerate leftovers.

Makes 6 servings.

One serving contains approximately: Calories 74, Fat 1g, Carbohydrates 17g, Protein 1g

Buttercup Squash with Apples Casserole

Serve this tasty buttercup squash side dish with turkey or ham.

Buttercup squash (about 3 pounds total), peeled, cut into medium-size pieces
¼ cup plus 2 tablespoons butter, divided
½ cup plus 1 tablespoon brown sugar, divided
¼ teaspoon salt
¼ teaspoon ground black pepper
⅛ teaspoon ground nutmeg

2 tablespoons margarine
6 cups peeled, cored and sliced Golden Delicious apples
¼ cup granulated sugar

1½ cups corn flakes dry cereal, crushed
½ cup coarsely chopped pecans
¼ teaspoon ground cinnamon

Preheat oven to 375°. Butter a 3-quart baking casserole.

Cover squash pieces with water in a large pot. Bring to a boil; cook until tender, about 15 minutes. Drain well. Add ¼ cup butter, 1 tablespoon brown sugar, salt, pepper and nutmeg; mash thoroughly in pot and set aside.

Melt margarine in a large nonstick skillet over low heat. Add apples and granulated sugar. Cover and cook over low heat, stirring occasionally, until tender but slightly firm. Spoon into prepared baking dish. Spread cooked squash evenly over apples.

Melt 2 tablespoons butter; place in a medium bowl. Add crushed cereal, pecans, ½ cup brown sugar and cinnamon; mix well. Sprinkle evenly over squash. Bake until thoroughly heated, about 15 minutes. Serve warm. Refrigerate leftovers.

Makes 8 servings.

One serving contains approximately: Calories 333, Fat 17g, Carbohydrates 50g, Protein 2g

Butternut Squash and Cranberries

My friend, KiKi, from Minnesota, loves butternut squash. This recipe is a great side.

1 medium-size butternut squash peeled, cut in half lengthwise, seeds
  discarded
4 tablespoons extra virgin olive oil, divided
Salt and ground black pepper to taste

2 medium-size yellow onions, peeled and cut into large chunks
Salt and black pepper to taste
2 tablespoons chopped sage
4 tablespoons dried cranberries

Preheat oven to 375°. Line 2 baking sheets with parchment paper.

Cut squash into large chunks; place in a bowl and coat with 2 tablespoons olive oil.
Season with salt and pepper to taste; place on one prepared baking sheet. Bake
about 30 minutes or until well caramelized.

Place onions in a bowl; coat with remaining 2 tablespoons olive oil. Season with
salt and pepper to taste; spread on second prepared baking sheet. Bake about
20 minutes or until well caramelized.

Place cooked squash and cooked onions in a bowl. Add sage and cranberries;
toss to combine. Serve immediately. Refrigerate leftovers.

Makes 4–6 servings.

One serving contains approximately: Calories 210, Fat 11g, Carbohydrates 29g, Protein 2g

Butternut Squash Fries

Serve this delicious side with ketchup.

1 2-pound fresh butternut squash
Salt to taste

Preheat oven to 425°.
Spray a baking sheet lightly with cooking spray.

Cut squash in half; discard seeds. Peel the squash.

Cut the peeled squash into sticks, like French fries. Place fries onto prepared baking sheet. Sprinkle with salt to taste.

Bake 10 minutes in preheated oven, then turn the fries over and continue baking about another 10 minutes or until edges are browned and slightly crisp. Remove from oven to a serving platter. Serve warm. Refrigerate leftovers.

Makes 4 servings.

Variation: Sprinkle cooked fries with garlic salt.

One serving contains approximately: Calories 107, Fat 0.5g, Carbohydrates 27g, Protein 2g

Butternut Squash-Pecan Casserole

This sweet, delicious side is so easy to prepare.

2 3-pound butternut squash

1 cup brown sugar, packed
2 eggs, beaten
½ cup butter, softened
½ teaspoon pure vanilla extract
¾ cup chopped pecans

Whole pecans, optional

Preheat oven to 350°. Grease a 2½-quart baking dish.

Cut squash in half lengthwise; discard seeds. Place squash in a baking pan, cut-side up. Add 1 inch water. Cover with aluminum foil. Bake until tender, about 1 hour. Remove from pan; cool slightly.

Remove pulp; place in a large bowl. Add sugar, eggs, butter and vanilla and mash together until blended. Spoon mixture into prepared baking dish. Top with whole pecans if desired.

Bake uncovered 45–50 minutes. Serve warm. Refrigerate leftovers.

Makes 8 servings.

One serving contains approximately: Calories 295, Fat 17g, Carbohydrates 36g, Protein 3g

Butternut Squash with Couscous

Garnish each serving with chopped almonds and chopped flat leaf parsley.

2 tablespoons extra virgin olive oil

1 cup diced yellow onion

3 cloves fresh garlic, finely chopped

1½ teaspoons salt, divided

1 teaspoon ground cumin, divided

⅛ teaspoon each: cinnamon, nutmeg, cayenne pepper

1 2-pound fresh butternut squash, halved, peeled, cut into 1-inch pieces

1 32-ounce container vegetable broth

1 15-ounce can chickpeas, drained

1 cup canned diced tomatoes

⅓ cup raisins

1½ cups water

1½ cups couscous

Heat olive oil in a large nonstick saucepot over medium heat. Add onion; stir and cook 5 minutes. Add garlic, 1 teaspoon salt, ½ teaspoon cumin, cinnamon, nutmeg and cayenne; stir and cook 1 minute.

Stir in squash, broth, chickpeas, tomatoes and raisins. Bring to a boil; reduce heat. Cover and simmer 10 minutes. Uncover and cook until squash is tender, about 20 minutes.

Bring water to a rolling boil in a medium saucepan. Stir in ½ teaspoon salt, ½ teaspoon cumin and couscous. Remove from heat and let stand 8 minutes. Fluff with a fork.

Spoon cooked couscous equally into individual bowls and top each with warm squash mixture. Serve warm. Refrigerate leftovers.

Makes 6 servings.

One serving contains approximately: Calories 325, Fat 1g, Carbohydrates 59g, Protein 10g

Cajun Squash French Fries

Great side with hot dogs or burgers! Serve with ketchup.

1 pound fresh butternut squash, peeled and
   cut into thick French fry-like pieces
½ teaspoon Cajun seasoning
¼ teaspoon salt
¼ teaspoon ground black pepper

Preheat oven to 450°. Spray a large baking sheet with cooking spray.

Place fries on prepared baking sheet, making sure to leave space between each piece. Sprinkle with seasonings.

Bake, turning each piece once, until tender and lightly browned, about 20 minutes. Remove from baking sheet. Serve. Refrigerate leftovers.

Makes 4 servings.

One serving contains approximately: Calories 52, Fat 0.5g, Carbohydrates 14g, Protein 1g

Chayote Rice Casserole

Serve this Mexican-flavored rice side dish warm.

1 cup chicken broth
½ cup extra long grain white rice
½ cup chopped yellow onion
1 teaspoon Mexican seasoning
1¼ cups purchased salsa, divided

1 large chayote squash
½ cup canned or frozen corn kernels
1 4-ounce can diced green chilies
1 cup shredded Mexican blend cheese

Preheat oven to 400°.

Stir broth, rice, onion, Mexican seasoning and ¼ cup salsa in a small saucepan. Bring mixture to a boil; cover and cook over low heat 20 minutes.

Peel squash, cut in half and discard pit. Chop squash and steam 5 minutes; drain well and set aside.

Spray a 1-quart baking dish with nonstick cooking spray. Layer half each of the rice mixture, chayote squash, corn, chilies, remaining salsa and cheese in baking dish; repeat layers.

Bake about 15 minutes or until cheese is melted and mixture is thoroughly heated. Serve. Refrigerate leftovers.

Makes 6 servings.

One serving contains approximately: Calories 170, Fat 6g, Carbohydrates 21g, Protein 6g

Cheddar Cheese and Yellow Squash Casserole

A delicious way to prepare yellow summer squash.

4 cups sliced fresh yellow squash
½ cup chopped yellow onion
1 cup water

3 dozen buttery round crackers, crushed
1 cup shredded Cheddar cheese

2 eggs, beaten in a small bowl
¾ cup whole milk
¼ cup butter, melted and cooled
¾ teaspoon salt
¼ teaspoon ground black pepper

2 tablespoons cold butter, cut into small pieces

Preheat oven to 400°. Lightly butter a 13x9-inch baking dish.

Place squash, onion and water in a skillet. Bring to a boil, then reduce heat. Cover and simmer 3 minutes. Drain well and place in a large bowl.

Mix crushed crackers and cheese in a another bowl; stir in half the mixture into the cooked squash. Stir in eggs, milk, melted butter, salt and pepper. Spoon mixture into prepared baking dish. Top with remaining cracker mixture. Dot with butter.

Bake about 25 minutes or until lightly browned. Serve warm. Refrigerate leftovers.

Makes 10 servings.

One serving contains approximately: Calories 200, Fat 16g, Carbohydrates 12g, Protein 6g

Cheese and Sour Cream Squash Bake

Sour cream lends a special flavor to this side dish.

1 2-pound butternut squash
1 cup water

6 buttery round crackers, crushed
1 tablespoon butter, melted

¾ cup shredded sharp Cheddar cheese
½ cup dairy sour cream
1 tablespoon chopped chives or green onions
¼ teaspoon salt, or to taste
¼ teaspoon ground white pepper
⅛ teaspoon smoked paprika

Preheat oven to 400°.

Cut squash lengthwise in half. Scoop out seeds. Place squash cut-side down in a 13x9-inch baking dish. Add water. Cover and bake until tender, about 40–60 minutes. Remove squash from baking dish; cool slightly. Scoop tender pulp into a medium bowl.

Add Cheddar cheese, sour cream, chives, salt, white pepper and paprika; mix well. Spoon mixture into a greased 2-quart baking dish.

Mix cracker crumbs and butter in a small bowl; sprinkle evenly over squash mixture. Bake until heated through, about 20–25 minutes. Serve warm. Refrigerate leftovers.

Makes 6 servings.

One serving contains approximately: Calories 180, Fat 11g, Carbohydrates 18g, Protein 5g

Cheesy Crookneck Yellow Squash Bake

Crookneck summer squash is a favorite in my garden.

2 tablespoons margarine
½ cup chopped yellow onion
4 crookneck yellow squash,
   cut into ¼-inch-thick slices

2 eggs
½ cup half-and-half or light cream
1¼ cups shredded sharp
   Cheddar cheese, divided
½ teaspoon salt

¼ teaspoon ground black pepper
¼ teaspoon dried thyme leaves
⅛ teaspoon ground nutmeg

2 cups 1-inch cubed
   French bread

Preheat oven to 375°. Grease an 8-inch-square glass baking dish.

Heat margarine in a 12-inch nonstick skillet over medium heat. Add onion; cook and stir 3 minutes. Add squash; cook and stir until tender, about 4 minutes. Remove from heat; set aside.

Beat eggs in a large bowl. Stir in half-and-half, ¾ cup cheese, salt, pepper, thyme and nutmeg. Add squash-onion mixture and bread cubes; stir to combine. Pour mixture into prepared baking dish.

Bake uncovered 25 minutes. Sprinkle with remaining cheese and continue baking about 10 minutes or until golden brown. Serve warm. Refrigerate leftovers.

Makes 4 servings.

One serving contains approximately: Calories 385, Fat 26g, Carbohydrates 21g, Protein 16g

Couscous with Zucchini

A delicious side to serve along with shrimp kabobs or other meats.

1 tablespoon extra virgin olive oil
2 cloves fresh garlic, minced

3 cups chicken broth
1 cup pimiento-stuffed green olives, cut into small pieces
1 10-ounce package quick-cooking couscous
3 medium-size fresh zucchini, cut lengthwise then very thinly sliced
2 teaspoons shredded fresh lemon peel
¼ teaspoon freshly ground black pepper, or to taste

4 green onions, thinly sliced
2 tablespoons coarsely chopped flat leaf parsley

Heat olive oil in a large saucepan. Add garlic; cook and stir 1 minute. Stir in broth and olives. Bring mixture to a boil. Stir in couscous, zucchini, lemon peel and black pepper.

Remove from heat. Cover and let stand 8 minutes.

Stir in green onions and parsley. Serve. Refrigerate leftovers.

Makes 8 servings.

Variation: Add grape tomatoes just before serving.

One serving contains approximately: Calories 198, Fat 5g, Carbohydrates 32g, Protein 6g

Cubed Butternut Squash Bake

Garlic and sage flavor this delicious side dish.

8 cups peeled, cubed butternut squash
1 tablespoon extra virgin olive oil

2 tablespoons butter
2 large cloves fresh garlic, minced
2 tablespoons chopped fresh sage
¼ teaspoon salt or to taste
¼ teaspoon ground black pepper or to taste

Preheat oven to 400°.

Place squash in 13x9-inch glass baking dish and toss with olive oil until coated.
Bake, stirring occasionally, until squash is tender when pierced with a fork, about
45–50 minutes.

Melt butter in a small saucepan. Add garlic and sage; cook and stir 2 minutes.
Pour over cooked squash and toss lightly. Season with salt and pepper. Serve.
Refrigerate leftovers.

Makes 9 servings.

One serving contains approximately: Calories 120, Fat 5g, Carbohydrates 22g, Protein 2g

Favorite Zucchini Bake

This Italian-flavored zucchini side dish will disappear fast.

3 tablespoons extra virgin
  olive oil, divided
7 cups ½-inch-sliced
  fresh zucchini
1 medium-size yellow onion,
  thinly sliced
2 large cloves garlic,
  finely chopped

1 28-ounce can diced tomatoes, undrained
1 teaspoon dried basil leaves
½ teaspoon dried oregano leaves
½ teaspoon salt
¼ teaspoon ground black pepper

1½ cups stuffing mix
½ cup grated Parmesan cheese
¾ cup shredded mozzarella cheese

Preheat oven to 350°. Grease a 13x9-inch baking dish.

Heat 1 tablespoon olive oil in a large nonstick skillet over medium heat. Add zucchini; cook and stir until tender, about 6 minutes. Remove from skillet to a bowl; set aside. Add remaining olive oil to same skillet; add onion and garlic. Cook and stir 2 minutes.

Add tomatoes, basil, oregano, salt and pepper. Reduce heat; simmer uncovered 10 minutes. Remove from heat. Stir in zucchini. Place mixture into prepared dish.

Top evenly with stuffing mix, then sprinkle with Parmesan cheese. Cover and bake 20 minutes.

Remove cover. Sprinkle top evenly with mozzarella cheese; bake uncovered until cheese melts, about 10 minutes. Remove from oven and let sit a few minutes before serving. Serve warm. Refrigerate leftovers.

Makes 6 servings.

One serving contains approximately: Calories 175, Fat 9g, Carbohydrates 17g, Protein 8g

Fresh Vegetable Sauté with Garlic Lemon Butter

Serve this tasty side with grilled or baked meat, poultry or fish.

3 tablespoons butter, divided
1½ tablespoons fresh lemon juice
2 cloves garlic, minced
2 tablespoons fresh herbs, such as rosemary, thyme, basil,
    parsley or marjoram

1 cup peeled baby carrots
Half of a medium-size red onion, peeled and cut into thin wedges
1 medium-size zucchini, sliced
1 medium-size crookneck yellow squash, sliced
1 red bell pepper, seeded and cut into thin matchstick strips
1 cup broccoli florets
Salt and black pepper to taste

Melt 2 tablespoons butter in a small saucepan. Add lemon juice and garlic; cook over low heat for 1 minute. Stir in herbs. Set aside and keep warm.

Melt 1 tablespoon butter in a large nonstick skillet. Add carrots and onion; cook and stir over medium-high heat until onion is soft, about 7 minutes. Add remaining vegetables; cook 5 minutes or until crisp-tender. Season with salt and pepper to taste.

Drizzle with garlic lemon butter; toss until coated. Serve. Refrigerate leftovers.

Makes 6 servings.

One serving contains approximately: Calories 80, Fat 6g, Carbohydrates 7g, Protein 1g

Glazed Patty Pan Squash, Carrots and Zucchini

Baby vegetables are delicious in this buttery glaze.

½ pound baby patty pan squash
½ pound baby carrots, trimmed and peeled
½ pound baby zucchini

3 tablespoons butter
2 teaspoons granulated sugar
½ teaspoon salt, or to taste
¼ teaspoon ground black pepper, or to taste
2 tablespoons chopped fresh dill

Steam vegetables in a steamer basket inside a covered saucepan until tender.

Melt butter in a large nonstick skillet over medium heat. Add steamed vegetables, sugar, salt and pepper; stir gently until heated through and glazed, about 4 minutes. Toss with dill. Serve warm. Refrigerate leftovers.

Makes 6 servings.

One serving contains approximately: Calories 90, Fat 6g, Carbohydrates 9g, Protein 1g

Hubbard Squash Bake

Hubbard squash is a special treat in this side dish.

10 cups peeled, 1-inch cubed Hubbard squash
2 firm pears, peeled and cored, cut into 1-inch pieces
1 cup cranberries
2 tablespoons butter
½ teaspoon salt
¼ teaspoon ground black pepper
2 tablespoons water

Preheat oven to 350°. Grease a 3-quart shallow baking dish.

Mix all ingredients in a large bowl. Pour into prepared baking dish.

Cover with aluminum foil. Bake 50–60 minutes or until squash is tender. Serve warm. Refrigerate leftovers.

Makes 14 servings.

One serving contains approximately: Calories 60, Fat 2g, Carbohydrates 11g, Protein 2g

Louisiana Sweet Potato Pumpkin Casserole

A great side for the holidays.

4 pounds sweet potatoes, peeled
  and cut into 2- to 3-inch pieces
1 15-ounce can pumpkin puree
  (not pie mix)
½ cup brown sugar, packed
3 tablespoons butter, softened
½ teaspoon salt
¼ teaspoon ground black pepper
2 large eggs
1 teaspoon pure vanilla extract

Topping:
⅓ cup brown sugar, packed
3 tablespoons all-purpose flour
1 tablespoon butter, melted
⅛ teaspoon salt
½ cup chopped pecans

Preheat oven to 350°. Lightly butter a 13x9-inch baking dish.

Microwave sweet potatoes on a microwave-safe plate until tender, about 15 minutes.
Cool slightly and place in a large bowl. Add pumpkin, ½ cup brown sugar, butter,
½ teaspoon salt and pepper. Mash with a potato masher until lumpy. Add eggs and
vanilla; stir until blended. Spoon mixture into prepared baking dish.

Topping: Mix brown sugar, flour, butter and salt in a bowl; sprinkle evenly over
mixture in baking dish. Sprinkle pecans evenly over the top.

Bake until thoroughly heated through, about 25 minutes. Place under the
broiler and broil until bubbly and nuts are toasted, about 1 minute. Serve warm.
Refrigerate leftovers.

Makes 18 servings.

One serving contains approximately: Calories 170, Fat 6g, Carbohydrates 28g, Protein 3g

Macaroni and Squash Casserole

Butternut squash is used in this creamy casserole.

2 tablespoons extra virgin olive oil
1 large yellow onion, thinly sliced
1 2-pound butternut squash, peeled, seeds discarded,
    cut into 1-inch pieces
1 15-ounce can coconut milk
Salt and black pepper to taste
1 tablespoon chopped fresh sage

12 ounces uncooked dried elbow macaroni
½ cup chopped toasted walnuts or pecans
½ cup bread crumbs

Preheat oven to 350°. Grease a 13x9-inch casserole baking dish.

Heat olive oil in medium nonstick pot over medium heat. Add onion; cook and stir until softened, about 5 minutes. Add squash, coconut milk, salt and pepper. Bring to a boil, then reduce heat to medium low. Cover and simmer until squash is tender, about 20 minutes. Stir in sage; simmer 1 minute.

Bring a large pot of salted water to a boil. Add macaroni; cook until firm-tender, about 8 minutes. Drain; rinse in cold water, then drain well and place in a large bowl. Add squash mixture, nuts, and salt and pepper to taste to bowl; mix well. Place mixture into prepared baking dish. Top with bread crumbs. Bake until hot throughout and golden brown. Serve warm. Refrigerate leftovers.

Makes 8 servings.

One serving contains approximately: Calories 430, Fat 19g, Carbohydrates 54g, Protein 11g

Microwave Squash Puree

Garnish this tasty side with snipped chives when serving.

1 2-pound winter squash, such as Hubbard, acorn or butternut,
   unpeeled, cut in half lengthwise and seeds discarded
4 tablespoons butter
1 tablespoon maple syrup
Salt to taste

Place squash skin up on a microwave-safe dish. Cover with microwave-safe plastic wrap. Microwave on high 6 to 8 minutes. Let rest until cool enough to handle. Carefully remove plastic wrap to avoid steam.

Scoop out pulp and place in a food processor. Add butter, syrup and salt to taste. Process until smooth. Spoon into a bowl. Refrigerate leftovers.

Makes 4 servings.

One serving contains approximately: Calories 160, Fat 12g, Carbohydrates 13g, Protein 2g

Rice Pilaf

Serve this colorful side dish with meats or seafood.

1 cup brown rice
2 cups low-sodium chicken broth

1 tablespoon extra virgin olive oil
½ cup cubed zucchini
½ cup cubed yellow summer squash
½ cup carrots cut into matchstick strips
2 cloves garlic, minced

¼ teaspoon freshly ground black pepper
1 teaspoon finely chopped flat leaf parsley

Cook rice in broth in a covered medium saucepan for 45 minutes. Cool uncovered
and set aside.

Heat olive oil in a large nonstick skillet over medium heat. Add zucchini, yellow
squash, carrots and garlic. Cook and stir until vegetables are crisp-tender.
Add cooked rice, black pepper and parsley. Stir and cook until thoroughly heated.
Serve warm. Refrigerate leftovers.

Makes 6 servings.

Variation: Use cooked long grain white rice.

One serving contains approximately: Calories 76, Fat 3g, Carbohydrates 12g, Protein 3g

Risotto with Buttercup Squash

Buttercup squash is delicious in this side dish.

6 cups chicken or vegetable stock

1 teaspoon extra virgin olive oil
3 tablespoons butter, divided
1 cup minced yellow onion
1 pound buttercup squash, peeled,
   seeded and cut into ½-inch dice

2 cups Arborio rice
½ cup dry white wine

½ cup grated Parmigiano-Reggiano
   cheese
Salt and freshly ground pepper
   to taste

Heat stock in a saucepan to a simmer while risotto is started.

Heat olive oil and 2 tablespoons butter and in a heavy-bottomed medium saucepan on low. Add onion and squash; stir. Cover and cook 10 minutes, stirring occasionally, to prevent sticking or browning, until onion is translucent and squash is tender.

Increase heat to medium. Add rice; stir to coat grains with butter. Cook 2 minutes.

Add wine; stir until evaporated, about 20 seconds.

Add 2 cups of the simmering stock; cook, stirring frequently, until liquid is almost absorbed.

Add more stock, 1 cup at a time, until rice is cooked al dente. (Each addition of stock should be almost absorbed before adding more. The amount of stock needed will vary. You may not use all 6 cups.)

Remove saucepan from heat. Stir in remaining butter and the cheese. Serve immediately. Refrigerate leftovers.

Makes 4 servings.

One serving contains approximately: Calories 420, Fat 15g, Carbohydrates 51g, Protein 11g

Roasted Delicata Squash with Potatoes

1 unpeeled large delicata squash (about 1½ pounds), washed,
   seeded and cut into 8 equal pieces.
4 medium-size butter potatoes, unpeeled, washed, quartered
4 cloves fresh garlic, crushed
¼ cup extra virgin olive oil
½ teaspoon salt or to taste
¼ teaspoon ground black pepper

Preheat oven to 425°.

Mix together squash, potatoes and garlic on a 13x9-inch baking sheet. Drizzle
evenly with olive oil. Season with salt and pepper.

Bake until tender, turning once after vegetables are browned, about 50 minutes.
Serve warm. Refrigerate leftovers.

Makes 8 servings.

Variation: Peel the delicata squash, if preferred.

One serving contains approximately: Calories 200, Fat 7g, Carbohydrates 32g, Protein 3g

Roasted Leeks and Patty Pan Squash

My friend Yvonne, from Rochester, New York, shares this simple side dish.

4 tablespoons basting oil, divided
3 8-ounce packages baby patty pan squash
1 8-ounce package cleaned and cut leeks
Salt and ground black pepper to taste

Preheat oven to 450°.

Coat bottom of a large shallow baking pan with 2 tablespoons basting oil.
Add squash and leeks; drizzle evenly with remaining 2 tablespoons basting oil.
Season with salt and black pepper to taste.

Roast 20–30 minutes or until squash and leeks are fork tender. Remove from oven and transfer to a serving dish. Serve warm. Refrigerate leftovers.

Makes 6 servings.

One serving contains approximately: Calories 100, Fat 6g, Carbohydrates 10g, Protein 2g

Roasted Sugar Pumpkin

Use mashed fresh pumpkin when making that special pie or other baked goods.

1 3-pound sugar pumpkin

Preheat oven to 375°.

Place whole pumpkin onto a baking sheet. Poke through top of pumpkin several times to vent steam while baking. Bake until fork tender, about 60 minutes. Remove pumpkin from oven and cool 30 minutes.

Cut pumpkin in half; discard seeds. Scrape cooked flesh from the skin and place in a bowl. Mash until smooth. If not using right away, cover and refrigerate for up to 2 days.

Makes 3 cups.

One serving contains approximately: Calories 45, Fat 0g, Carbohydrates 11g, Protein 2g

Saucy Parmesan Zucchini

Serve with warm garlic bread.

1 pound thinly sliced fresh zucchini (about 4 medium)
8 ounces fresh button mushrooms, thinly sliced
1 cup prepared spaghetti sauce
1 cup shredded part-skim mozzarella cheese
¼ cup grated Parmesan cheese

Preheat oven to 400°. Coat a 13x9-inch baking dish with cooking spray.

Mix zucchini, mushrooms and sauce in a bowl; spoon into prepared baking dish.

Bake 25 minutes, then sprinkle evenly with cheeses and continue baking until cheese is melted, about 5 minutes. Serve. Refrigerate leftovers.

Makes 6 servings.

One serving contains approximately: Calories 110, Fat 6g, Carbohydrates 8g, Protein 8g

Spaghetti Squash Bake

Serve with a crisp green salad and warm garlic bread for a tasty lunch.

1 medium-size spaghetti squash
1 cup cold water

1 tablespoon extra virgin olive oil
1 tablespoon butter
8 ounces sliced fresh button
    mushrooms
1 cup chopped yellow onion
3 cloves garlic, finely chopped
½ teaspoon dried oregano

½ teaspoon dried basil
¼ teaspoon dried thyme
½ teaspoon salt
¼ teaspoon ground black pepper
2 fresh tomatoes, chopped
1 cup dried bread crumbs
1 cup ricotta cheese
¼ cup finely chopped fresh flat
    leaf parsley
¼ cup grated Parmesan cheese

Preheat oven to 375°. Grease a 2-quart baking dish.

Cut squash in half lengthwise; discard seeds. Place squash cut-side down in a rimmed baking pan; add water. Cover with aluminum foil. Bake until tender, about 30 minutes. Remove from pan. Remove pulp, separating strands of squash with a fork; place in a large bowl and set aside.

Heat olive oil and butter in a large nonstick skillet. Add mushrooms, onion, garlic, oregano, basil, thyme, salt and pepper. Cook and stir until onion is tender. Stir in tomatoes; cook, stirring often, 5 minutes. Add to bowl with squash. Stir in bread crumbs, ricotta cheese and parsley. Spoon mixture into prepared baking dish; sprinkle top evenly with Parmesan cheese.

Bake uncovered about 45 minutes or until thoroughly heated and top is slightly browned. Serve hot. Refrigerate leftovers.

Makes 6 servings.

One serving contains approximately: Calories 270, Fat 9g, Carbohydrates 37g, Protein 18g

Spaghetti Squash Bake with Cheese and Fresh Spinach

Serve as a side or a complete meal along with a tossed salad and rolls.

1 3-pound spaghetti squash, cut in half lengthwise, seeds discarded

1 tablespoon extra virgin olive oil

1 15-ounce container ricotta cheese

1 egg

4 cups fresh baby spinach, coarsely chopped

2 cloves fresh garlic, chopped

1 teaspoon salt

½ teaspoon ground black pepper

⅛ teaspoon ground nutmeg, optional

2 cups grated mozzarella cheese

Preheat oven to 400°. Lightly oil a rimmed baking sheet.

Drizzle cut sides of squash with olive oil, then place cut-side down on prepared baking sheet. Bake until tender, about 40 minutes. Remove from oven; cool slightly. With a fork, gently remove the cooked strands of pulp from shell of squash. Place in a large bowl.

Add ricotta, egg, spinach, garlic, salt, pepper and nutmeg to the bowl; gently mix to combine. Spoon mixture into an 8-inch-square baking dish. Sprinkle top with mozzarella. Bake until browned and bubbly, about 20 minutes. Serve warm. Refrigerate leftovers.

Makes 8 servings.

One serving contains approximately: Calories 245, Fat 16g, Carbohydrates 13g, Protein 14g

Spaghetti Squash with Sauce

Garnish each serving with thinly sliced fresh basil leaves.

1 large spaghetti squash, cut in
  half lengthwise, seeds discarded
1 tablespoon extra virgin olive oil
½ cup chopped yellow onion
⅛ teaspoon crushed red
  pepper flakes
2 cloves fresh garlic, finely
  chopped

1 sprig fresh rosemary
1½ cups canned Italian-style
  tomatoes with juice, crushed
¼ cup water
Salt and black pepper to taste

4 teaspoons grated
  Romano cheese

Place squash, one half at a time, cut-side down on a microwave-safe dish.
Cover with microwave-safe plastic wrap. Microwave on high for 10–12 minutes or
until tender.

Let rest, covered, 15 minutes or until cool enough to handle. Carefully remove
plastic wrap. Run a fork lengthwise over cooked cut surface of squash to remove
spaghetti-like strands; place in a bowl and set aside.

Heat olive oil in a large nonstick skillet on medium-low. Add onion and pepper
flakes; cook and stir until onion is softened but not brown. Add garlic; cook and stir
2 minutes. Add rosemary, tomatoes, water and salt and pepper to taste. Simmer
on low heat 10 minutes. Discard rosemary.

Add cooked squash strands; toss quickly to coat and heat thoroughly. Top with
cheese when serving. Refrigerate leftovers.

Makes 9 servings.

One serving contains approximately: Calories 45, Fat 2g, Carbohydrates 6g, Protein 1g

Streusel-Topped Butternut Squash Casserole

This casserole is a delicious accompaniment to ham or turkey . . . or hot dogs!

¾ cup granulated sugar
⅓ cup butter or margarine
2 large eggs
1 5-ounce can evaporated milk
2 cups cooked mashed butternut squash
1 teaspoon pure vanilla extract

½ cup crisped rice cereal
¼ cup brown sugar, packed
½ cup chopped pecans
2 tablespoons butter or margarine, melted and cooled

Preheat oven to 350°. Grease a 11x7-inch casserole dish.

Beat granulated sugar and ⅓ cup butter in a large bowl until light and fluffy. Beat in eggs. Gradually beat in evaporated milk. Stir in squash and vanilla extract until blended. Pour mixture into prepared baking dish. Bake until almost set, about 40–45 minutes. Remove from oven.

Mix together rice cereal, brown sugar, pecans and 2 tablespoons melted butter in a small bowl; sprinkle evenly over squash in baking dish. Return to oven and continue baking until bubbly, about 10 minutes. Serve warm. Refrigerate leftovers.

Makes 6 servings.

One serving contains approximately: Calories 298, Fat 18g, Carbohydrates 38g, Protein 4g

Stuffed Mini Pumpkins

You will love the looks of this tasty side . . . great for Thanksgiving Day.

½ cup uncooked wild rice
3 to 4 cups cold water or
   as needed

4 fresh mini pumpkins

1 teaspoon fresh orange zest
Juice of 1 large fresh orange
2 tablespoons honey
½ teaspoon salt, or to taste
¼ teaspoon ground black pepper
¼ cup dried cranberries
2 tablespoons chopped
   pecans, toasted
1 teaspoon fresh chopped mint

Preheat oven to 375°.

Place wild rice in a small saucepan. Cover with water. Bring to a boil over medium-high heat, then reduce heat to low and simmer for about 40 minutes or until done (the rice is done when the grains start to pop). Pour cooked rice into a colander and rinse with cold water; drain. Place drained rice in a large bowl.

While the rice is cooking, cut tops off of pumpkins. Scoop out seeds and strings. Place pumpkins cut-side down in a baking pan with ½ inch of water. Bake 15 minutes in preheated oven. Remove from oven. Turn pumpkins upright, then return to oven and bake until tender when flesh is pierced with a fork, about 10 minutes. Remove from pan to a large platter.

Mix orange zest, orange juice, honey, salt, pepper, cranberries, pecans and mint in a small bowl; add to rice in bowl and mix well. Stuff rice mixture into cooked pumpkins. Serve warm. Refrigerate leftovers.

Makes 4 servings.

One serving contains approximately: Calories 170, Fat 3g, Carbohydrates 35g, Protein 5g

Summer Squash Lasagna

My dear niece, Terri, shares this summer squash lasagna recipe.

9 uncooked lasagna noodles
(8 ounces)
2 tablespoons cooking oil
2 crookneck yellow squash,
cut into ½-inch pieces
1 medium-size zucchini, cut
into ½-inch pieces
1 large red bell pepper,
chopped

½ pound fresh button mushrooms, sliced
3 large cloves garlic, finely chopped
1 15-ounce container fat-free ricotta cheese
2 cups mozzarella cheese, divided
½ cup grated Parmesan cheese
1 egg
½ teaspoon freshly ground black pepper
½ teaspoon dried oregano leaves
1 28-ounce jar light spaghetti sauce

Preheat oven to 375°. Lightly grease a 13x9-inch baking dish.

Cook lasagna noodles following package directions, omitting salt; drain. Set aside.

Heat cooking oil in a large nonstick skillet over medium-high heat. Add yellow squash, zucchini, bell pepper, mushrooms and garlic. Cook and stir until tender, about 5 minutes. Remove from heat; set aside.

Mix ricotta, 1½ cups mozzarella, Parmesan, egg, black pepper and oregano in a large bowl until blended. Spread one-third of the spaghetti sauce evenly over bottom of prepared baking dish. Place 3 noodles over sauce, then spread one-third of cheese mixture over noodles. Spoon with one-third of the vegetable mixture. Repeat layers two more times; top with remaining ½ cup mozzarella cheese.

Cover with aluminum foil. Bake 45 minutes. Remove foil and continue baking about 12 minutes or until heated through and cheese is golden. Remove from oven and let rest a few minutes before serving. Refrigerate leftovers.

Makes 8 servings.

One serving contains approximately: Calories 325, Fat 7g, Carbohydrates 40g, Protein 25g

Summer Stir-Fried Zucchini

Variation: Use crookneck yellow squash along with zucchini for a colorful dish.

¼ cup extra virgin olive oil
8 small zucchinis, unpeeled, thinly sliced (about 2 pounds)
¾ teaspoon salt or to taste
2 cloves fresh garlic, finely chopped

¼ teaspoon dried oregano leaves
¼ teaspoon dried basil leaves

Heat olive oil in a large nonstick skillet over medium-high heat. Add zucchini; sprinkle with salt. Stir and cook 2 minutes. Add garlic; stir and cook 3 minutes or until zucchini is crisp-tender. Sprinkle with oregano and basil. Serve. Refrigerate leftovers.

Makes 8 servings.

One serving contains approximately: Calories 80, Fat 7g, Carbohydrates 4g, Protein 1g

Sweet Potato and Butternut Mash

A sweet side to serve with most meats.

3 sweet potatoes, peeled and cut into small pieces
1 butternut squash, peeled, seeded and cut into small pieces

¼ teaspoon salt, or to taste
¼ teaspoon ground black pepper
½ teaspoon ground cinnamon
¼ teaspoon ground nutmeg
½ teaspoon pure vanilla extract
¼ cup maple syrup

Place sweet potatoes and squash in a large saucepan. Add enough water to cover. Bring to a boil, then reduce heat. Cover and simmer until tender, about 20 minutes. Drain well and place into a bowl. Mash until smooth.

Stir in remaining ingredients until blended. Serve warm. Refrigerate leftovers.

Makes 4 servings.

Variation: Omit syrup, add 2 tablespoons soft butter.

One serving contains approximately: Calories 80, Fat 0.5g, Carbohydrates 19g, Protein 2g

Two-Cheese Butternut Squash Gratin

Two cheeses make this butternut gratin special.

1 small butternut squash, peeled (about 1½ pounds)
2 large slices thick-cut bacon, cut crosswise into ¼-inch pieces
1 medium-size red onion, cut into ¼-inch slices
2 teaspoons chopped fresh sage
2 teaspoons chopped fresh thyme
¼ teaspoon coarse salt
1 teaspoon ground black pepper
1¼ cups shredded Swiss cheese
¼ cup heavy cream
½ cup shredded Parmesan cheese
½ cup toasted bread crumbs

Preheat oven to 400°. Butter an 8x8-inch baking dish.

Cut squash in half lengthwise; discard seeds. Cut across into ¼-inch thick slices.

Cook bacon in a skillet over medium heat until brown and crisp; remove bacon and drain on paper towels. Discard all but 1 tablespoon bacon drippings. Add onion to skillet. Cook and stir over medium-high heat until onion is soft but not brown, about 5 minutes. Add sage and thyme; mix well.

Place half of the squash slices in prepared baking dish. Sprinkle with salt and pepper. Spread half of the onions and half of the bacon over squash. Repeat layers. Top with Swiss cheese. Pour cream around edges of gratin. Cover loosely with aluminum foil. Bake about 35 minutes or until squash is tender. Remove foil. Sprinkle with Parmesan cheese and top with bread crumbs.

Reduce heat to 375°. Bake uncovered about 15 minutes or until cheeses are melted and bread crumbs are golden brown. Let stand 15 minutes before serving. Refrigerate leftovers.

Makes 6 servings.

One serving contains approximately: Calories 320, Fat 19g, Carbohydrates 26g, Protein 14g

Walnut and Ginger Butternut Squash

Variation: Use pecans instead of walnuts.

1 2-pound butternut squash, peeled, seeded and 1-inch cubed
1 tablespoon cooking oil
¼ teaspoon salt

1 cup walnuts
3 tablespoons butter
2 teaspoons grated ginger
1 teaspoon vanilla extract
½ teaspoon dried thyme
Black pepper to taste
Lemon juice to taste

Preheat oven to 400°.

Toss the squash with oil and spread on a baking sheet. Sprinkle with salt; roast about 20 minutes, until tender and starting to brown. Remove from oven.

Toast the walnuts in a large sauté pan over medium heat, stirring frequently, until fragrant and starting to brown. Add butter to pan; toss to coat walnuts with melted butter. Add squash and toss again. Add ginger, vanilla extract, thyme and black pepper and toss once more.

Remove from heat and sprinkle with lemon juice. Serve. Refrigerate leftovers.

Makes 6 servings.

One serving contains approximately: Calories 260, Fat 20g, Carbohydrates 15g, Protein 6g

Winter Squash Gratin

Garnish this delicious side dish with chopped flat leaf parsley when serving.

1 2-pound fresh butternut squash

¼ cup butter
3 cloves garlic, finely chopped

¼ teaspoon salt
¼ teaspoon ground black pepper
¼ teaspoon dried oregano leaves

¼ cup coarse unflavored dried bread crumbs, such as panko
¼ cup grated Parmesan cheese

Preheat oven to 375°. Lightly grease a 13x9-inch glass baking dish.

Peel squash then cut in half lengthwise; discard seeds. Cut into ½-inch-thick slices. Place slices overlapping slightly in prepared baking dish.

Melt butter in a small saucepan over low heat. Add garlic; cook and stir 3 minutes. Set aside 1 tablespoon of mixture. Brush squash slices with remaining mixture. Sprinkle with salt, pepper and oregano.

Mix bread crumbs, cheese and 1 tablespoon reserved butter mixture in a bowl; sprinkle evenly over squash. Bake until squash is tender and slightly browned, about 1 hour. Serve warm. Refrigerate leftovers.

Makes 6 servings.

One serving contains approximately: Calories 185, Fat 10g, Carbohydrates 18g, Protein 4g

Winter Squash Holiday Casserole

Serve this sweet side for special holiday dinners.

1 large butternut squash (about
   3 pounds), peeled, seeded
   and cut into small pieces
1 cup whole milk
8 tablespoons butter,
   melted, divided
3 eggs, slightly beaten
¾ cup granulated sugar
1 teaspoon pure vanilla extract

1 scant teaspoon ground cinnamon
⅛ teaspoon ground cloves
⅛ teaspoon ground nutmeg
¼ cup all-purpose flour

½ cup crushed sugar cookies
   or vanilla wafers
¼ cup brown sugar, packed
2 tablespoons chopped pecans

Preheat oven to 350°. Grease a 2-quart baking dish.

Place squash in a large saucepan with enough water to cover. Bring to a boil, then reduce heat. Cover and cook until tender, 20–30 minutes. Drain well. Place squash in a large bowl; beat or mash until smooth. Stir in milk, 6 tablespoons melted butter, eggs, granulated sugar and vanilla until very well blended. Mix cinnamon, cloves, nutmeg and flour together in a bowl; stir into squash mixture until blended.

Spoon mixture into prepared dish. Cover with aluminum foil and bake 45 minutes. Remove from oven. Remove foil.

In a small bowl, mix together cookies, brown sugar, pecans and 2 tablespoons melted butter; sprinkle evenly over casserole. Return to oven and bake uncovered 10–12 minutes or until heated through. Serve warm. Refrigerate leftovers.

Makes 8 servings.

One serving contains approximately: Calories 290, Fat 14g, Carbohydrates 44g, Protein 4g

Zesty Yellow Summer Squash Casserole

Garnish this Tex-Mex style casserole with thinly sliced green onions and coarsely chopped red onion when serving.

10 cups quartered and thinly sliced yellow summer squash
1 cup finely chopped yellow onion
1 4-ounce can chopped green chilies
½ teaspoon chopped seeded fresh jalapeno, more if you like it hot
½ teaspoon salt or to taste
¼ teaspoon ground black pepper
2¼ cups grated extra sharp Cheddar cheese, divided
¼ cup all-purpose flour

¾ cup purchased mild salsa

Preheat oven to 400°. Lightly grease a 13x9-inch baking dish.

Mix together yellow squash, onion, chilies, jalapeno, salt, pepper and ¾ cup cheese in a large bowl. Add flour; mix well. Spread mixture into prepared dish.

Cover with aluminum foil and bake until squash is tender, about 45 minutes. Remove from oven; spread salsa on top, then sprinkle with remaining cheese. Return to oven; bake uncovered until golden, about 30 minutes. Serve warm. Refrigerate leftovers.

Makes 12 servings.

One serving contains approximately: Calories 110, Fat 5g, Carbohydrates 9g, Protein 5g

Zucchini and Fresh Corn Cakes

Serve plain or with sour cream.

3 medium-size zucchinis, cored, seeded and shredded (about 5 cups)
2 cups fresh corn kernels (about 2 ears)
2 green onions, chopped
2 tablespoons chopped fresh oregano
1 cup tempura batter mix or 1½ cups all-purpose baking mix
1 teaspoon salt
½ teaspoon ground black pepper
2 large eggs
¼ cup cold water

3 tablespoons cooking oil, divided

Mix all ingredients except cooking oil in a large bowl until well blended.

Heat 1 tablespoon cooking oil in a large nonstick skillet over medium-high heat.

Drop four ½-cup portions of batter onto heated skillet and spread each portion with the back of a spoon to form 3-inch pancakes. Cook about 3 minutes, then turn and cook other side an additional 2 minutes. Keep warm on a serving platter.

Repeat, following same procedure as above, until all batter is gone. Serve warm. Refrigerate leftovers.

Makes 6 servings.

One serving contains approximately: Calories 210, Fat 10g, Carbohydrates 26g, Protein 5g

Zucchini Cheese Rice Bake

Two of my favorite ingredients, rice and cheese, are in this zucchini side dish.

3 medium-size unpeeled zucchini,
   cut into ⅛-inch slices

3 cups cooked long grain white rice
1 4-ounce can chopped green chilies
4 cups shredded Monterey Jack
   cheese, divided
2 cups dairy sour cream
2 tablespoons chopped green
   bell pepper

2 tablespoons chopped onion
1 tablespoon minced fresh flat
   leaf parsley
1 teaspoon dried oregano leaves
1 teaspoon salt
¼ teaspoon ground black pepper

2 medium-size ripe tomatoes, sliced

Preheat oven to 350°. Grease a shallow 3-quart baking dish.

Place zucchini in a large saucepan with ½-inch water. Bring to a boil. Reduce heat; cover and simmer until zucchini is crisp-tender, about 5 minutes. Drain well; set aside.

Place cooked rice in prepared baking dish. Layer with chilies and 1½ cups cheese.

In a large bowl, mix together sour cream, bell pepper, onion, parsley, oregano, salt and black pepper. Spread over cheese. Layer with zucchini and tomato. Sprinkle with remaining cheese.

Cover and bake 30 minutes. Uncover and bake until heated through and cheese is melted, about 10 minutes. Remove from oven; let stand a few minutes before serving. Refrigerate leftovers.

Makes 12 servings.

One serving contains approximately: Calories 290, Fat 18g, Carbohydrates 17g, Protein 12g

Zucchini Parmesan Rounds

Serve this delicious side dish for a special lunch.

2 medium unpeeled fresh zucchini
1 tablespoon extra virgin olive oil

½ cup freshly grated Parmesan cheese (about 2 ounces)
½ cup plain dry bread crumbs
⅛ teaspoon salt
Freshly ground black pepper to taste
Paprika to taste

Preheat oven to 450°. Lightly coat a baking sheet with nonstick cooking spray.

Slice zucchini into ¼-inch rounds; place in a plastic food bag. Add olive oil; shake to coat well.

Mix together cheese, bread crumbs, salt, pepper and paprika in a small bowl. Press each zucchini round into mixture, coating both sides. Place in a single layer on prepared baking sheet.

Bake until browned and crisp, about 10 minutes. Remove with a spatula. Serve warm. Refrigerate leftovers.

Makes 4 servings.

One serving contains approximately: Calories 140, Fat 7g, Carbohydrates, 13g, Protein, 7g

Breads

Banana-Winter Squash Quick Bread

Winter squash, such as butternut or Hubbard, makes delicious bread.

3 cups all-purpose flour
2 cups granulated sugar
2 teaspoons baking soda
1½ teaspoons baking powder
1 teaspoon salt
1½ teaspoons ground cinnamon
¼ teaspoon ground ginger
¼ teaspoon ground cloves

3 eggs
1 cup cooking oil
2 teaspoons pure vanilla extract
1 cup cooked winter squash
1 cup mashed ripe bananas
1 cup chopped walnuts or pecans

Preheat oven to 350°. Grease two 8x4-inch loaf baking pans.

Mix flour, sugar, baking soda, baking powder, salt, cinnamon, ginger and cloves in a large bowl; set aside.

Beat eggs in another bowl. Stir in cooking oil, vanilla extract, squash and bananas; add mixture to flour mixture and stir until just moistened. Fold in walnuts. Pour batter equally into prepared baking pans.

Bake about 1 hour or until a wooden pick inserted in the center comes out clean. Cool in pan for 10 minutes. Remove from pan; cool on a wire rack. Serve. Refrigerate leftovers.

Makes 2 loaves.

One serving contains approximately: Calories 190, Fat 10g, Carbohydrates 24g, Protein 3g

Buttercup Squash Bread

Enjoy this buttercup squash bread warm or at room temperature.

1 package active dry yeast (¼ ounce)
½ cup warm water (110°–115°)
2 tablespoons molasses
1 teaspoon salt
1 teaspoon caraway seeds
1 cup mashed cooked buttercup squash
3 cups all-purpose flour, divided

In a large bowl, mix yeast with warm water until dissolved. Add molasses, salt, caraway seeds, squash and 2 cups flour; mix well. Add enough remaining flour to form soft dough. Place dough on a floured surface; knead until smooth and elastic, about 8 minutes.

Place dough in a large greased bowl, turning once to grease top. Cover with a clean kitchen towel and let rise until doubled in size, about an hour. Punch dough down and place on a floured surface. Shape into a loaf. Place in a greased 9x5-inch loaf baking pan. Cover with a clean kitchen towel and let rise until doubled in size, about 45 minutes.

Preheat oven to 400°.

Bake bread 25–30 minutes or until golden brown. Remove from oven and immediately remove from pan. Cool on a wire rack. Refrigerate leftovers.

Makes 16 servings.

One serving contains approximately: Calories 100, Fat (trace amount), Carbohydrates 21g, Protein 3g

Butternut Squash Cloverleaf Rolls

Serve these rolls for a special Thanksgiving dinner treat . . . or any time!

¼ cup warm water, 110°–115°
2 tablespoons granulated sugar
1 package active dry yeast (¼ ounce)

1 cup warm whole milk, 110°–115°
4 tablespoons butter, melted and
  cooled, divided

1 teaspoon salt
1 cup mashed cooked
  butternut squash
¾ cup shredded mild
  Cheddar cheese
4 to 4½ cups all-purpose
  flour, approximately

Stir water and sugar in a large bowl until sugar is dissolved. Stir in yeast. Let stand in a warm place until foamy, about 5 minutes. Stir in milk, 3 tablespoons butter, salt, squash and Cheddar cheese. Add about 4 cups of flour to form soft dough.

Knead dough on a floured surface about 5 minutes or until no longer sticky, adding a little more flour if needed. Form dough into a ball; place in a well-greased bowl, turning once to grease top. Cover with a clean kitchen towel and let rise in a warm place until doubled in size, about 1 hour.

Preheat oven to 375°. Grease 24 regular-size muffin cups.

Punch down dough. Break off three small pieces of dough at a time and roll each into a 1-inch ball. Place three balls in each muffin cup. Cover with a clean kitchen towel and let rise in a warm place until doubled in size, about 30 minutes. Gently brush tops with 1 tablespoon cooled melted butter. Bake about 15–18 minutes. Serve warm.

Makes 24 rolls.

Variation: Use sharp Cheddar cheese.

One serving contains approximately: Calories 120, Fat 3g, Carbohydrates 19g, Protein 3g

Cheddar Zucchini Drop Biscuits

Great served with fresh tomato soup.

2 cups all-purpose flour
1 tablespoon baking powder
¾ teaspoon salt
⅛ teaspoon ground red pepper, or to taste
1 cup shredded sharp Cheddar cheese

¾ cup shredded fresh zucchini
⅔ cup whole milk
¼ cup butter, melted

Preheat oven to 450°. Coat a baking sheet with nonstick cooking spray.

Mix flour, baking powder, salt and red pepper in a medium bowl until well blended. Stir in cheese.

Mix zucchini, milk and butter in a small bowl; add to flour mixture and stir, just until moistened. Drop batter by heaping tablespoons onto prepared baking sheet.

Bake 12–15 minutes or until golden brown. Serve warm. Refrigerate leftovers.

Makes 12 servings.

One serving contains approximately: Calories 160, Fat 7g, Carbohydrates 17g, Protein 5g

Chocolate Chip Pumpkin Bread

Variation: Use regular semi-sweet chocolate chips.

4 cups all-purpose flour
2 teaspoons baking soda
1 teaspoon salt
1 teaspoon ground cinnamon
½ teaspoon ground nutmeg

2 cups granulated sugar
¾ cup butter or margarine, softened
4 eggs

1 15-ounce can pumpkin puree
  (not pie mix)
1 teaspoon pure vanilla extract
½ cup cold water

1 cup miniature semi-sweet
  chocolate chips
¼ cup chopped pecans

Preheat oven to 350°. Grease and flour only the bottoms of two 8x4-inch loaf baking pans.

Mix flour, baking soda, salt, cinnamon and nutmeg in a medium bowl; set aside.

Beat sugar and butter in a large mixer bowl on medium speed until creamy. Beat in eggs. Reduce speed to low. Beat in pumpkin, vanilla extract and water. Add flour mixture; beat until just moistened. Stir in chocolate chips and pecans. Spread batter into prepared pans.

Bake 65–75 minutes or until a wooden pick inserted in center comes out clean. Cool in pans for 10 minutes. Remove from pans; cool on a wire rack. Serve. Refrigerate leftovers.

Makes 2 loaves.

One serving contains approximately: Calories 200, Fat 7g, Carbohydrates 30g, Protein 3g

Chocolate Zucchini Bread

Share a loaf with a friend.

1 cup butter
4 1-ounce squares semi-sweet
  baking chocolate
1½ cups granulated sugar
1½ cups unpeeled fresh zucchini
4 eggs
1 teaspoon pure vanilla extract

1¾ cup all-purpose flour
1 teaspoon baking powder
½ teaspoon baking soda
½ teaspoon salt

1 teaspoon ground cinnamon
⅛ teaspoon ground cloves
½ cup chopped walnuts

Glaze:
1½ ounces white chocolate,
  melted, mixed in a small bowl
  with 2 teaspoons cooking oil

Preheat oven to 350°. Grease and flour two 8x4-inch loaf baking pans.

Melt butter and baking chocolate in a 2-quart saucepan over medium-low heat, stirring occasionally. Remove from heat. Stir in sugar, zucchini, eggs and vanilla.

Stir flour, baking powder, baking soda, salt, cinnamon, cloves and walnuts in a large bowl until well mixed. Add zucchini mixture and stir just to moisten. Spoon batter equally into prepared pans.

Bake 35–45 minutes or until a wooden pick inserted in center comes out clean. Cool in pan for 10 minutes. Remove from pan; cool completely on a wire rack. Drizzle glaze over cooled bread. Serve. Refrigerate leftovers.

Makes 2 loaves.

One serving contains approximately: Calories 220, Fat 13g, Carbohydrates 24g, Protein 3g

Favorite Pumpkin Pecan Bread

Share a loaf with your neighbor . . . they will love it!

¼ cup butter
¼ cup margarine
1 8-ounce package cream
   cheese, softened
2½ cups granulated sugar
4 eggs
1 15-ounce can pumpkin (not pie mix)
1 teaspoon pure vanilla extract

3½ cups all-purpose flour
2 teaspoons baking soda

½ teaspoon baking powder
1 teaspoon salt
1 scant teaspoon
   ground cinnamon
¼ teaspoon ground cloves
⅛ teaspoon ground ginger

1 cup coarsely chopped pecans

Preheat oven to 350°. Grease and flour two 9x5-inch loaf baking pans.

Beat butter, margarine, cream cheese and sugar in a large mixer bowl on medium speed until creamy. Beat in eggs one at a time. Beat pumpkin and vanilla on low speed to blend.

Mix flour, baking soda, baking powder, salt, cinnamon, cloves and ginger in a medium bowl until well blended. Add to mixture in mixer bowl, a little at a time, and beat on low until blended. Stir in pecans by hand. Pour batter equally into prepared pans.

Bake 55–60 minutes or until a wooden pick inserted in center comes out clean. Cool completely on a wire rack before serving. Refrigerate leftovers.

Makes 32 servings.

One serving contains approximately: Calories 200, Fat 9g, Carbohydrates 28g, Protein 3g

Oatmeal Pumpkin Bread

Spread a slice of this delicious bread with apple jelly . . . enjoy.

1 cup uncooked quick-cooking oats
1 cup milk, heated
¾ cup canned pumpkin puree
  (not pie mix)
2 eggs, beaten
¼ cup margarine, melted and
  cooled
1 teaspoon pure vanilla extract, optional

2 cups all-purpose flour
1 cup granulated sugar
1 tablespoon baking powder
¼ teaspoon salt
1 teaspoon ground cinnamon
¼ teaspoon ground nutmeg
⅛ teaspoon ground cloves

1 cup raisins
½ cup chopped pecans

Preheat oven to 350°. Grease a 9x5-inch loaf baking pan.

Mix oats and milk in a large bowl; let stand 5 minutes. Stir in pumpkin, eggs, margarine and vanilla extract.

Mix flour, sugar, baking powder, salt, cinnamon, nutmeg, and cloves in another bowl; gradually stir mixture into oat mixture.

Stir in raisins and pecans. Spread batter into prepared baking pan.

Bake 55–60 minutes or until a wooden pick inserted in center comes out clean. Cool in pan for 5 minutes. Remove from pan; cool on a wire rack. Serve. Refrigerate leftovers.

Makes 1 loaf.

One serving contains approximately: Calories 227, Fat 7g, Carbohydrates 39g, Protein 5g

Pumpkin-Carrot-Raisin Bread

Serve this delicious bread warm or at room temperature.

3 cups all-purpose flour
5 teaspoons pumpkin pie spice
2 teaspoons baking soda
1½ teaspoons salt

3 cups granulated sugar
1 15-ounce can pumpkin (not pie mix)
4 eggs
1 cup cooking oil
½ cup water
1 teaspoon pure vanilla extract

1 cup shredded carrots
1 cup raisins

Preheat oven to 350°. Grease and flour two 9x5-inch loaf baking pans.

Mix flour, pumpkin pie spice, baking soda and salt in a large bowl.

Beat sugar, pumpkin, eggs, cooking oil, water and vanilla in a large mixer bowl; beat on medium speed until just blended. Add mixture to flour mixture; stir just enough to moisten.

Stir in carrots and raisins. Spoon batter equally into prepared baking pans.

Bake 60–65 minutes or until a wooden pick inserted in center comes out clean. Cool in pans on a wire rack for 10 minutes. Remove from pans; cool on a wire rack. Slice and serve. Refrigerate leftovers.

Makes 2 loaves.

One serving contains approximately: Calories 270, Fat 10g, Carbohydrates 44g, Protein 3g

Pumpkin Seed Breadsticks

Purchased pizza dough is used to make these quick breadsticks.

1 14-ounce package refrigerated pizza dough
1 egg, beaten
3 tablespoons shelled pumpkin seeds
Coarse salt

Preheat oven to 425°. Lightly grease two large baking sheets.

Unroll pizza dough on a lightly floured surface. Use your hands to shape dough into a 12x9-inch rectangle. Brush dough with some of the egg. Sprinkle with seeds and lightly sprinkle with salt. Use a floured pizza cutter to cut dough crosswise into ½-inch-wide strips. Place strips onto prepared baking sheets.

Bake one sheet at a time for 8–10 minutes or until golden brown. Remove from pan; cool on a wire rack. Serve. Refrigerate leftovers.

Makes 24 breadsticks.

Variation: Mix black sesame seeds with the pumpkin seeds.

One serving contains approximately: Calories 39, Fat 1g, Carbohydrates 6g, Protein 1g

Pumpkin Scones

Offer these scones for breakfast with cinnamon honey butter.

½ cup butter, softened
½ cup brown sugar, packed
1 cup canned pumpkin
   (not pie mix)
¼ cup whole milk
1 egg yolk
½ teaspoon pure vanilla extract

2½ cups all-purpose flour
2 teaspoons baking powder
½ teaspoon salt

1 teaspoon ground cinnamon
½ teaspoon ground ginger
½ teaspoon ground cloves
½ cup golden raisins

Glaze:
1 cup powdered sugar
½ teaspoon pure vanilla extract
1 to 2 tablespoons fresh orange juice

Preheat oven to 375°.

Beat butter and brown sugar in a large bowl on medium speed until creamy. Add pumpkin, milk, egg yolk and ½ teaspoon vanilla extract; beat until blended.

In a medium bowl, mix together flour, baking powder, salt and spices; add to butter mixture until blended. Stir in raisins. Drop dough by rounded ¼-cupfuls onto an ungreased baking sheet. Bake 20–25 minutes or until edges are lightly browned and scones are set. Remove from baking sheet. Cool on a wire rack.

Mix powdered sugar, vanilla and enough orange juice to make a desired glazing consistency. Drizzle over baked scones. Refrigerate leftovers.

Makes 12 scones.

One serving contains approximately: Calories 260, Fat 8g, Carbohydrates 42g, Protein 4g

Summer Squash Cornbread

Serve warm with honey butter . . . great with ham and beans.

2 pounds yellow summer squash (about 5 medium), chopped
2 8½-ounce packages cornbread muffin mix
4 eggs, lightly beaten
⅔ cup cottage cheese
½ cup shredded Cheddar cheese
½ cup finely chopped yellow onion
¼ teaspoon salt
¼ teaspoon ground black pepper

Preheat oven to 400°. Grease an 8-inch-square baking pan.

Place squash in a steamer basket; place in a large saucepan with 1-inch-deep water. Bring to a boil; cover and steam for 5 minutes or until squash is tender. Drain and squeeze dry.

In a large bowl, combine cornbread mix and eggs. Fold in squash, cottage cheese, Cheddar cheese, onion, salt and pepper. Pour mixture into prepared baking pan.

Bake 20–25 minutes or until a wooden pick inserted in the center comes out clean. Cool in pan for 10 minutes. Remove from pan; cool on a wire rack. Refrigerate leftovers.

Makes 24 servings.

One serving contains approximately: Calories 116, Fat 4g, Carbohydrates 17g, Protein 4g

Zucchini Bread

Slice and freeze one loaf for another day.

3 cups all-purpose flour
1 teaspoon salt
1 teaspoon baking soda
¼ teaspoon baking powder
1 tablespoon ground cinnamon
¼ teaspoon ground nutmeg
¼ teaspoon ground cloves

2 cups granulated sugar
1 cup butter, softened
3 eggs
2 teaspoons pure vanilla extract

2 cups shredded fresh zucchini
½ cup chopped walnuts

Preheat oven to 350°. Grease only the bottoms of two 8x4-inch loaf baking pans.

Mix together flour, salt, baking soda, baking powder, cinnamon, nutmeg and cloves in a large bowl; set aside.

Beat sugar, butter, eggs and vanilla in a large mixer bowl on medium speed. Reduce speed to low; add flour mixture to bowl and beat until well mixed. Stir in zucchini and walnuts. Spoon batter equally into prepared baking pans.

Bake 55–65 minutes or until a wooden pick inserted in the center comes out clean. Cool in pans for 10 minutes. Remove from pans; cool on a wire rack. Serve. Refrigerate leftovers.

Makes 2 loaves.

One serving contains approximately: Calories 220, Fat 10g, Carbohydrates 30g, Protein 3g

Zucchini Dinner Rolls

Zucchini rolls for dinner . . . the gang will be coming soon!

1 cup shredded peeled fresh zucchini
1 teaspoon salt, divided
3½ cups all-purpose flour, divided
1 package (¼ ounce) quick-rise yeast
5 tablespoons grated Parmesan cheese, divided
1 teaspoon granulated sugar

1 cup warm water (120° to 130°)
¼ cup butter, softened

Place zucchini in a bowl; sprinkle with ½ teaspoon salt and let stand 5 minutes; drain well.

In a large bowl, mix together 3 cups flour, yeast, 2 tablespoons cheese, sugar and ½ teaspoon salt, then add drained zucchini and toss to combine.

Mix together water and butter in a small bowl; add to flour mixture. Stir in remaining flour to form soft dough. Place dough on a well-floured surface and knead until smooth and elastic, about 8 minutes. Place dough in a greased bowl, turning once to grease top. Cover with a clean kitchen towel and let rise until doubled in size, about 1 hour.

Divide dough in half. Shape each half into 12 smooth balls. Place in a greased 13x9-inch baking pan. Sprinkle with remaining cheese. Repeat. Cover and let rise until doubled in size, about 45 minutes. Preheat oven to 375°. Bake rolls 20–25 minutes or until golden brown. Remove from pan to a wire rack. Serve warm.

Makes 24 servings.

One serving contains approximately: Calories 90, Fat 2g, Carbohydrates 14g, Protein 3g

Muffins

Carrot-Zucchini Muffins

Serve these warm muffins plain or with orange marmalade.

¾ cup orange juice
½ cup butter, melted and cooled
1 egg plus 1 egg white, beaten
1 teaspoon pure vanilla extract

1 cup all-purpose flour
1 cup whole wheat flour
½ cup granulated sugar
1 teaspoon baking powder
½ teaspoon baking soda
½ teaspoon salt
1 teaspoon ground cinnamon

1 cup shredded carrots
1 cup shredded fresh zucchini

Preheat oven to 400°. Grease a 12-cup muffin pan.

Mix orange juice, butter, eggs and vanilla in a large bowl.

Mix remaining ingredients, except carrots and zucchini, in a medium bowl; add to orange juice mixture and stir just until moistened.

Stir in carrots and zucchini. Spoon batter equally into prepared muffin cups.

Bake 20–25 minutes or until a wooden pick inserted in the center comes out clean. Cool in the pan for 5 minutes, then remove and cool on a wire rack. Refrigerate leftovers.

Makes 12 muffins.

One serving contains approximately: Calories 190, Fat 8g, Carbohydrates 27g, Protein 3g

Chocolate Chip Pumpkin Muffins

These muffins are sure become a favorite . . . add chopped walnuts for extra goodness.

1½ cups all-purpose flour
1½ cups whole wheat flour
2 teaspoons baking soda
2 teaspoons baking powder
½ teaspoon salt
1½ teaspoons ground cinnamon
¼ teaspoon ground ginger
¼ teaspoon ground cloves

4 eggs, slightly beaten
2 cups granulated sugar
1 15-ounce can pumpkin (not pie mix)
1 cup cooking oil
¼ cup milk
1 teaspoon pure vanilla extract

1 12-ounce package semi-sweet
  chocolate chips

Preheat oven to 400°. Grease 36 2½-inch muffin baking cups, or line with paper muffin liners.

Mix first eight ingredients in a medium bowl.

Stir eggs, sugar, pumpkin, oil, milk and vanilla in another bowl until blended. Add to flour mixture; stir just enough to moisten. Stir in chocolate chips. Spoon batter equally into prepared muffin cups.

Bake 20–25 minutes or until tops spring back when touched. Cool in the pan for 5 minutes. Remove from pan; cool on a wire rack. Serve. Refrigerate leftovers.

Makes 36 muffins.

One serving contains approximately: Calories 200, Fat 10g, Carbohydrates 26g, Protein 3g

Yellow Summer Squash Muffins

This is a great way to use the abundant crop of summer squash . . . so delicious.

1 pound yellow summer squash, cut into 1-inch pieces
½ cup butter, melted
1 egg, lightly beaten

1½ cups all-purpose flour
½ cup granulated sugar
2½ teaspoons baking powder
½ teaspoon salt

Preheat oven to 375°. Grease a 12-cup muffin pan.

Add 1 inch of water to a medium saucepan; add squash and bring to a boil.
Reduce heat. Cover pan and simmer 5 minutes or until squash is tender. Drain
squash; place in a bowl and mash. Stir in butter and egg.

Mix together flour, sugar, baking powder and salt; add to squash mixture and stir
just to moisten. Fill prepared muffin cups three-quarters full.

Bake 20–25 minutes or until a wooden pick inserted in the center comes
out clean. Cool in pan for 5 minutes. Remove from pan; cool on a wire rack.
Refrigerate leftovers.

Makes 12 servings.

One serving contains approximately: Calories 170, Fat 8g, Carbohydrates 22g, Protein 3g

Zucchini Chocolate Chip Muffins

Serve these muffins slightly warm . . . with a tall glass of milk.

1½ cups all-purpose flour
2 tablespoons uncooked oat bran
¾ cup granulated sugar
1 teaspoon baking soda
½ teaspoon salt
1 teaspoon ground cinnamon

1 cup shredded fresh zucchini
½ cup semi-sweet chocolate chips
¼ cup chopped walnuts, optional

2 eggs, beaten
½ cup cooking oil
¼ cup milk
1 teaspoon pure vanilla extract

Preheat oven to 400°. Line a 12-cup muffin pan with paper muffin liners.

Mix flour, oat bran, sugar, baking soda, salt and cinnamon in a large bowl.

Stir together eggs, cooking oil, milk and vanilla extract in a small bowl; add to flour mixture and stir just to moisten.

Stir in zucchini, chocolate chips and walnuts. Fill prepared muffin cups two-thirds full with batter.

Bake about 20–25 minutes. Remove from oven. Remove muffins from pan and cool on a wire rack. Refrigerate leftovers.

Makes 12 muffins.

One serving contains approximately: Calories 231, Fat 12g, Carbohydrates 28g, Protein 3g

Cakes

Ali's Pumpkin Crumb Cake

Serve plain or with whipped topping as desired.

1 30-ounce can pumpkin pie mix
1 5-ounce can evaporated milk
2 large eggs, slightly beaten in a small bowl
1 teaspoon pure vanilla extract

1 18.25-ounce package yellow cake mix
1 stick butter or margarine, melted
½ cup chopped pecans

Preheat oven to 350°. Grease a 13x9-inch baking pan.

Mix together pumpkin pie mix, evaporated milk, eggs and vanilla extract in a large bowl until well blended. Pour mixture into prepared baking pan.

On low speed, with an electric mixer, mix together cake mix, melted butter and pecans in a large bowl until crumbly (or use clean hands to mix). Sprinkle mixture over filling in pan.

Bake 50–55 minutes or until top is golden brown. Remove pan from oven. Cool completely in pan on a wire rack. Cut into bars. Serve. Refrigerate leftovers.

Makes 20 servings.

One serving contains approximately: Calories 230, Fat 11g, Carbohydrates 31g, Protein 3g

Chocolate Chip Zucchini Cake

Serve plain or frost with your favorite frosting.

1½ cups granulated sugar
½ cup butter or margarine, softened
¼ cup cooking oil
1 teaspoon pure vanilla extract
2 eggs

2½ cups all-purpose flour
¼ cup unsweetened baking cocoa
1 teaspoon baking soda
½ cup buttermilk

2 cups unpeeled shredded fresh zucchini
¾ cup semi-sweet chocolate chips
½ cup chopped walnuts, optional

Preheat oven to 350°. Grease and flour a 13x9-inch baking pan.

Beat sugar, butter, cooking oil, vanilla and eggs in a large bowl until well blended.

Mix together flour, cocoa and baking soda in medium bowl; add to butter mixture. Stir until well blended. Stir in zucchini, chocolate chips and walnuts. Pour batter into prepared baking pan.

Bake 35–45 minutes or until a wooden pick inserted in the center comes out clean. Cool completely in pan. Serve. Refrigerate leftovers.

Makes 16 servings.

One serving contains approximately: Calories 280, Fat 12g, Carbohydrates 39g, Protein 4g

Chocolate Cucuzza Squash Cake

Cucuzza (pronounced guh-GOO-tza) is a long green Italian squash with white pulp.

½ cup butter, softened
½ cup cooking oil
1¾ cups granulated sugar
2 eggs
2 teaspoons pure vanilla extract

¼ cup unsweetened baking cocoa
1 teaspoon baking soda
½ teaspoon baking powder
½ teaspoon salt
½ teaspoon ground cinnamon

¼ teaspoon ground cloves
½ cup buttermilk
2 cups unpeeled shredded
  cucuzza squash

6 tablespoons butter, softened
⅔ cup brown sugar, packed
1 cup sweetened coconut
½ cup chopped pecans
¼ cup whole milk
½ teaspoon pure vanilla extract

Preheat oven to 325°. Grease a 13x9-inch baking pan.

Beat butter, oil and sugar in a large mixer bowl until smooth. Beat in eggs, then beat in 2 teaspoons vanilla extract.

Mix together baking cocoa, baking soda, baking powder, salt, cinnamon and cloves; add to creamed mixture, alternately with buttermilk. Stir in cucuzza; pour into prepared pan. Bake 45–50 minutes or until a wooden pick inserted in the center comes out clean. Cool in pan on a wire rack for 10 minutes.

Mix together last 6 ingredients in a bowl. Spread over warm cake. Broil in oven about 4–6 inches from heat for 2 minutes. Cool cake completely. Serve. Refrigerate leftovers.

Makes 15 servings.

One serving contains approximately: Calories 433, Fat 24g, Carbohydrates 54g, Protein 4g

Chocolate Zucchini Cake

Sprinkle with powdered sugar when serving, and serve with vanilla ice cream.

½ cup butter
½ cup cooking oil
1¾ cups granulated sugar
2 eggs
½ cup buttermilk
1 teaspoon pure vanilla extract

2 cups all-purpose flour
1 teaspoon baking soda
½ teaspoon salt
¾ teaspoon ground cinnamon
¼ teaspoon ground cloves
¼ cup unsweetened cocoa powder

2½ cups unpeeled grated zucchini

¼ cup finely chopped walnuts
¼ cup semi-sweet chocolate chips

Preheat oven to 350°. Grease and flour a 13x9-inch baking pan.

Beat butter, oil and sugar in a large mixer bowl until light. Beat in eggs, buttermilk and vanilla extract.

Mix together flour, baking soda, salt, cinnamon, cloves and cocoa powder in a medium bowl; add to butter mixture and mix well. Stir in zucchini; mix well. Pour batter into prepared baking pan. Sprinkle with walnuts and chocolate chips.

Bake about 40–45 minutes. Cool in the pan on a wire rack. Serve.
Refrigerate leftovers.

Makes 16 servings.

One serving contains approximately: Calories 260, Fat 14g, Carbohydrates 33g, Protein 3g

Easy Zucchini Cake Squares

This is another way to use those garden zucchinis . . . so delicious.

3 eggs
¾ cup cooking oil
2 teaspoons pure vanilla
   extract, divided
2 cups all-purpose flour
2 cups granulated sugar
2 teaspoons baking powder
1½ teaspoons salt
1 teaspoon ground cinnamon
2 cups shredded fresh zucchini

1 3-ounce package cream
   cheese, softened
2 tablespoons butter, softened
3 cups powdered sugar
2 to 3 tablespoons fresh orange juice

Preheat oven to 350°. Grease a 15x10x1-inch baking pan.

In a large bowl, beat eggs, oil and 1 teaspoon vanilla extract. In a small bowl, mix together flour, sugar, baking powder, salt and cinnamon; stir into egg mixture. Stir in zucchini; mix well. Spread into prepared baking pan.

Bake 20–25 minutes or until a wooden pick inserted in the center comes out clean. Cool completely in the pan on a wire rack.

In a small bowl, beat cream cheese, butter and 1 teaspoon vanilla extract. Gradually beat in powdered sugar. Add enough orange juice to form a spreading consistency. Frost cooled cake. Cut into squares. Store in the refrigerator.

Makes 24 servings.

One serving contains approximately: Calories 255, Fat 10g, Carbohydrates 40g, Protein 2g

Frosted Butternut Squash Cake

Variation: Omit frosting. Sprinkle with powdered sugar. Serve with ice cream.

1½ cups granulated sugar
1¼ cups butter, divided
3 eggs

2½ cups all-purpose flour
1½ teaspoons baking powder
½ teaspoon baking soda
½ teaspoon salt
¾ teaspoon ground cinnamon
½ teaspoon ground ginger
¼ teaspoon ground nutmeg

¾ cup buttermilk
2 cups shredded peeled
   butternut squash
½ cup chopped pecans

1 3-ounce package cream cheese,
   softened
4 cups powdered sugar
½ teaspoon pure vanilla extract
2 to 4 tablespoons orange juice
½ cup finely chopped pecans

Preheat oven to 350°. Grease only the bottom of a 13x9-inch baking pan.

Beat granulated sugar and ¾ cup butter on medium speed in a large mixer bowl until light and fluffy. Beat in eggs. Mix together flour, baking powder, baking soda, salt, cinnamon, ginger and nutmeg in a medium bowl; add to butter mixture, alternately with buttermilk. Beat until blended, about 1 minute. Stir in squash and pecans. Bake about 40 minutes or until a wooden pick inserted in the center comes out clean. Cool completely in pan.

Beat ½ cup butter and cream cheese with an electric mixer in a medium bowl until creamy. Add powdered sugar, vanilla extract and enough orange juice to make a desired frosting consistency. Frost cake; sprinkle with pecans. Store covered in the refrigerator.

Makes 15 servings.

One serving contains approximately: Calories 534, Fat 24g, Carbohydrates 72g, Protein 6g

Pumpkin-Apple Bundt Cake

Serve this gingerbread-flavored cake with vanilla ice cream for extra goodness.

Hard sauce:
½ cup butter, softened
1 teaspoon vanilla extract
2 cups powdered sugar

3½ cups all-purpose flour
1 tablespoon baking powder
2½ teaspoons ground ginger
½ teaspoon pumpkin pie spice
½ teaspoon baking soda
½ teaspoon salt

1 cup butter or margarine, softened
1 cup granulated sugar
½ cup brown sugar, packed
4 large eggs
1 15-ounce can pumpkin (not pie mix)
1 cup shredded, peeled tart apple
½ cup molasses
1 teaspoon pure vanilla extract

Preheat oven to 350°. Grease and flour a 12-cup bundt baking pan.

Hard Sauce: Beat ½ cup butter, 1 teaspoon vanilla and powdered sugar in a medium bowl until fluffy. Set aside.

In a medium bowl, mix together flour, baking powder, ginger, pie spice, baking soda and salt in a medium bowl; set aside. In a larger mixer bowl, beat butter, granulated sugar and brown sugar until creamy. Beat in eggs, one at a time. Beat in pumpkin, apple, molasses and 1 teaspoon vanilla. On low speed, gradually beat in flour mixture. Spoon batter into prepared baking pan.

Bake 55–50 minutes or until a wooden pick inserted in the center comes out clean. Cool in pan on a wire rack 15 minutes; invert onto a serving plate. Dust with powdered sugar before serving. Serve warm with hard sauce. Refrigerate leftovers.

Makes 12 servings.

One serving contains approximately: Calories 460, Fat 18g, Carbohydrates 70g, Protein 7g

Pumpkin Coconut Snack Cake

A great snack cake.

1 18.25-ounce package yellow cake mix, divided
2 large eggs
1⅔ cups pumpkin pie mix
2 teaspoons pumpkin pie spice
1 teaspoon pure vanilla extract

½ cup flaked coconut
¼ cup chopped pecans or walnuts
3 tablespoons butter or margarine, softened

Preheat oven to 350°. Grease a 13x9-inch baking pan.

In a large bowl, mix together 3 cups dry cake mix, eggs, pumpkin pie mix, pumpkin pie spice and vanilla extract; beat on low speed until moistened, then beat on medium speed for 2 minutes. Pour into prepared baking pan.

In a small bowl, mix together coconut, pecans and remaining dry cake mix. Cut in butter with a pastry blender or 2 knives until crumbly. Sprinkle mixture over batter.

Bake 30–35 minutes or until a wooden pick inserted in the center comes out clean. Cool in pan on a wire rack. Refrigerate leftovers.

Makes 20 servings.

One serving contains approximately: Calories 170, Fat 6g, Carbohydrates 26g, Protein 3g

Pumpkin Dump Cake

Dump cakes are easy to prepare. Serve in small dessert bowls with vanilla ice cream.

1 15-ounce can pumpkin (not pie mix)
1 cup granulated sugar
1½ teaspoons ground cinnamon
1 teaspoon ground ginger
½ teaspoon ground cloves
½ teaspoon salt
1 12-ounce can evaporated milk
1 teaspoon pure vanilla extract
4 eggs

1 18.25-ounce package
   yellow cake mix
1 cup chopped pecans
½ cup butter, melted

Preheat oven to 350°. Grease and flour a 13x9-inch baking pan.

In a large bowl, stir together pumpkin, sugar, cinnamon, ginger, cloves and salt until blended. Stir in evaporated milk and vanilla extract. Beat in eggs, one at a time. Pour mixture into prepared pan.

Sprinkle dry cake mix over pumpkin mixture, then sprinkle evenly with pecans and drizzle evenly with butter.

Bake 50–60 minutes or until edges are lightly browned. Cool in the pan on a wire rack.

Serve warm or at room temperature. Refrigerate leftovers.

Makes 12 servings.

One serving contains approximately: Calories 448, Fat 22g, Carbohydrates 59g, Protein 7g

Pumpkin Pound Cake

Homemade pumpkin pound cake is a special dessert.

3¾ cups all-purpose flour
1½ teaspoons baking powder
1 teaspoon baking soda
1 teaspoon salt
2 teaspoons pumpkin pie spice

2 cups granulated sugar
1½ cups butter, softened
   (no substitution)
6 eggs

¾ cup canned pumpkin (not pie mix)
1 teaspoon pure vanilla extract
¾ cup whole milk

Glaze:
1½ cups powdered sugar
3 tablespoons butter, softened
¼ teaspoon pure vanilla extract
4 to 6 teaspoons fresh orange juice,
   or as needed to make a
   drizzling consistency

Preheat oven to 350°. Grease and flour a 12-cup bundt baking pan.

Mix together first 5 ingredients in a medium bowl; set aside.

Beat granulated sugar and 1½ cups butter with an electric mixer in a large mixer bowl on medium speed until creamy. Beat in eggs, one at a time. Beat in pumpkin and 1 teaspoon vanilla extract. Reduce speed to low. Gradually beat in flour mixture, alternately with milk, until well mixed. Spoon batter into prepared baking pan.

Bake 55–60 minutes or until a wooden pick inserted in the center comes out clean. Cool in pan 10 minutes. Remove from pan; cool completely. Glaze; serve. Refrigerate leftovers.

Glaze: Mix all glaze ingredients in a small bowl. Glaze cooled cake.

Makes 16 servings.

One serving contains approximately: Calories 460, Fat 22g, Carbohydrates 60g, Protein 6g

Pumpkin Sheet Cake with Cream Cheese Frosting

Serve plain or with a scoop of cinnamon ice cream.

1½ cups granulated sugar
1 15-ounce can pumpkin (not pie mix)
1 cup cooking oil
4 eggs

2 cups all-purpose flour
2 teaspoons baking powder
¼ teaspoon salt
2 teaspoons ground cinnamon
¼ teaspoon ground ginger
⅛ teaspoon ground cloves

1 8-ounce package cream
 cheese, softened
½ cup butter, softened
1½ teaspoons vanilla extract
5 cups powdered sugar

Preheat oven to 350°. Grease a 15x10x1-inch baking pan.

Beat granulated sugar, pumpkin, cooking oil and eggs in a large bowl.

Mix together flour, baking powder, salt, cinnamon, ginger and cloves in a medium bowl; add to pumpkin mixture and mix well. Pour batter into prepared pan. Bake 20–25 minutes or until a wooden pick inserted in the center comes out clean. Cool completely in pan on a wire rack.

Beat cream cheese, butter and vanilla in medium bowl. Gradually beat in powdered sugar until smooth. Spread over cooled cake. Store covered in the refrigerator.

Makes 24 servings.

One serving contains approximately: Calories 340, Fat 16g, Carbohydrates 49g, Protein 3g

Winter Squash Coffee Cake

Invite the neighbor over for coffee and this special cake.

1 cup powdered sugar
1½ teaspoons vanilla, divided
Juice from 1 orange
1¼ cup granulated sugar
¼ cup brown sugar, packed
2¼ cups all-purpose flour, divided
¼ cup uncooked quick oats
¼ cup chopped pecans
3 tablespoons cold butter, cut
   into small pieces

2½ teaspoons ground
   cinnamon, divided
½ cup margarine, or butter
2 eggs
1 cup mashed cooked butternut squash
2 teaspoons baking powder
½ teaspoon salt
¼ teaspoon each: ground ginger,
   ground nutmeg, ground cloves
½ cup unsweetened applesauce

Preheat oven to 350°. Grease a 9-inch springform baking pan.
Glaze: In a small bowl, mix powdered sugar, ½ teaspoon vanilla and enough
orange juice, adding a little at a time, to make a drizzling consistency.

Mix ¼ cup granulated sugar, brown sugar, ¼ cup flour, oats, pecans, butter and
1 teaspoon cinnamon in a bowl until crumbly; set aside. Beat margarine and 1 cup
granulated sugar in a large mixer bowl on medium speed until light and creamy.
Beat in eggs, squash and 1 teaspoon vanilla. Mix together 2 cups flour, baking
powder, salt, 1½ teaspoons cinnamon, ginger, nutmeg and cloves in a medium
bowl; gradually beat into creamed mixture on low speed until blended.

Spoon half the mixture into prepared baking pan. Spread applesauce over batter.
Sprinkle with half the crumbly mixture. Top with remaining batter. Sprinkle with
remaining crumbly mixture. Bake about 55 minutes or until a wooden pick
inserted in the center comes out clean. Cool in pan 10 minutes; remove sides.
Cool completely. Drizzle with glaze. Refrigerate leftovers.

Makes 10 servings.

One serving contains approximately: Calories 354, Fat 14g, Carbohydrates 53g, Protein 5g

Cupcakes

Double Chocolate Zucchini Cupcakes

Serve plain, or frost with purchased chocolate frosting.

½ cup butter, softened
½ cup cooking oil
1¾ cups granulated sugar
2 eggs
½ cup whole milk
1 teaspoon pure vanilla extract

2½ cups all-purpose flour
¼ cup unsweetened cocoa powder
1 teaspoon baking soda
½ teaspoon salt

½ teaspoon ground cinnamon
⅛ teaspoon ground cloves

2 cups unpeeled shredded fresh zucchini
¼ cup miniature semi-sweet chocolate chips
¼ cup chopped pecans or walnuts

Preheat oven to 375°. Line 24 muffin cups with paper muffin liners.

In a large mixer bowl, beat butter, oil and sugar until fluffy. Beat in eggs, milk and vanilla extract until blended.

In a medium bowl, mix together flour, cocoa powder, baking soda, salt, cinnamon and cloves; on low speed, gradually add to creamed mixture. Stir in zucchini and chocolate chips with a spoon. Fill prepared muffin cups two-thirds full.

Bake 20–25 minutes or until a wooden pick inserted in the center comes out clean. Cool in pans 10 minutes; remove from pan and cool on a wire rack. Refrigerate leftovers.

Makes 24 cupcakes.

One serving contains approximately: Calories 210, Fat 11g, Carbohydrates 27g, Protein 3g

Frosted Chocolate Zucchini Cupcakes

The kids will love 'em!

2½ cups all-purpose flour
¾ cup unsweetened baking
   cocoa powder
1 teaspoon baking powder
1 teaspoon baking soda
½ teaspoon salt

1½ cups granulated sugar
1¼ cups butter, softened
2 eggs
1 teaspoon pure vanilla extract

½ cup buttermilk
2 cups grated fresh zucchini
¼ cup raisins

1 16-ounce can purchased
   chocolate frosting

Preheat oven to 350°. Line 24 muffin cups with paper muffin liners.

Mix together flour, cocoa, baking powder, baking soda and salt in a bowl; set aside.

Beat sugar and butter in a large mixer bowl with an electric mixer until light and fluffy. Beat in eggs, one at a time. Beat in vanilla. On low speed, gradually beat in flour mixture alternately with buttermilk. Fold in zucchini and raisins. Spoon batter equally into prepared baking cups.

Bake 20–25 minutes or until a wooden pick inserted in the center comes out clean. Cool in pan 10 minutes. Remove from pan; cool completely. Frost. Refrigerate leftovers.

Makes 24 cupcakes.

One serving contains approximately: Calories 320, Fat 17g, Carbohydrates 40g, Protein 3g

Frosted Pumpkin Cupcakes

Cream cheese-frosted pumpkin cupcakes are perfect for any occasion.

2⅓ cups all-purpose flour
1 teaspoon baking powder
½ teaspoon baking soda
½ teaspoon salt
1 tablespoon pumpkin spice
½ teaspoon ground cinnamon
¼ teaspoon ground

2½ cups granulated sugar
¾ cup butter, softened
3 eggs

1 15-ounce can pumpkin puree
  (not pie mix)
1 teaspoon pure vanilla extract
1 cup buttermilk

Frosting:
1 8-ounce package cream cheese,
  softened
½ cup butter, softened
4 cups powdered sugar
1 teaspoon vanilla extract

Preheat oven to 350°. Line 24 muffin cups with paper muffin liners.

Mix together first 7 ingredients in a medium bowl; set aside.

Beat granulated sugar and ¾ cup butter in a large mixer bowl on medium speed until light and fluffy. Beat in eggs, one at a time. Beat in pumpkin and 1 teaspoon vanilla extract. Gradually beat in flour mixture alternately with buttermilk. Spoon batter into prepared muffin cups, filling each three-quarters full.

Bake 20–25 minutes or until a wooden pick inserted in the center comes out clean. Cool in muffin pan 10 minutes. Remove from pan. Cool completely.
Beat all frosting ingredients in a bowl until creamy. Frost. Refrigerate leftovers.

Makes 24 cupcakes.

One serving contains approximately: Calories 340, Fat 14g, Carbohydrates 53g, Protein 4g

Pumpkin Cream Cupcakes

A cake mix is use to make these cupcakes. Serve plain or dust with powdered sugar.

1 package (2-layer size) spice cake mix
1 ¾-ounce package vanilla flavor instant pudding mix
1 cup canned pumpkin (not pie mix)

1 8-ounce package cream cheese, softened
¼ cup granulated sugar
1 egg
1 teaspoon pure vanilla extract

Preheat oven to 350°. Line 24 muffin cups with paper muffin liners.

Prepare cake batter following package directions. Add dry pudding mix and pumpkin; mix well. Spoon into prepared muffin cups.

Beat cream cheese in a medium mixer bowl with an electric mixer until creamy. Beat in sugar, egg, and vanilla extract until well blended; spoon mixture equally over batter.

Bake 18–22 minutes or until a wooden pick inserted in the center comes out clean. Cool in pan 5 minutes; remove and cool completely on a wire rack. Store in the refrigerator.

Makes 24 cupcakes.

One serving contains approximately: Calories 190, Fat 9g, Carbohydrates 25g, Protein 3g

Raspberry-Zucchini-Chocolate Cupcakes

Top each cupcake with a fresh raspberry and a mint leaf when serving.

2½ cups all-purpose flour
¼ cup unsweetened cocoa powder
1 teaspoon baking soda
1 teaspoon baking powder
½ teaspoon salt

1 cup granulated sugar
¾ cup butter, softened
2 eggs
1 teaspoon pure vanilla extract
½ cup buttermilk
2 cups shredded fresh zucchini
1¼ cups fresh raspberries
1 cup semi-sweet chocolate chips

Preheat oven to 350°. Grease 24 muffin cups or line with paper muffin liners.

Mix together flour, cocoa powder, baking soda, baking powder and salt in a bowl; set aside.

Beat sugar and butter in a large mixer bowl on medium speed until light and fluffy. Beat in eggs one at a time; beat in vanilla extract. On low speed, gradually beat in flour mixture alternately with buttermilk. Fold in zucchini, raspberries and chocolate chips.

Spoon batter equally into prepared baking cups, filling three-quarters full.

Bake 20–25 minutes or until a wooden pick inserted in the center comes out clean. Cool in pan 10 minutes. Remove from pan; cool on a wire rack. Serve. Refrigerate leftovers.

Makes 24 cupcakes.

One serving contains approximately: Calories 180, Fat 9g, Carbohydrates 25g, Protein 2g

Cheesecakes

Butternut Squash Cheesecake

Use baked acorn squash puree instead of butternut.

1 10-inch unbaked pie crust

1 8-ounce package cream cheese, softened
2 eggs
1 cup baked butternut squash puree
1 cup milk
1 teaspoon stevia liquid sweetener
¼ teaspoon salt
½ teaspoon ground cinnamon
⅛ teaspoon ground nutmeg
⅛ teaspoon ground ginger
⅛ teaspoon allspice
1 teaspoon pure vanilla extract

Preheat oven to 350°. Line a 10-inch deep-dish pie plate with pie crust.

Beat cream cheese in a large mixer bowl until smooth. Beat in eggs and squash puree. Beat in remaining ingredients until well blended. Pour mixture into pie crust.

Bake 40 to 45 minutes or until set. Cool on a wire rack. Serve. Store in the refrigerator.

Makes 8 servings.

Variation: Use appropriate amount granulated sugar instead of liquid sweetener.

One serving contains approximately: Calories 216, Fat 15g, Carbohydrates 16g, Protein 4g

Praline Pumpkin Cheesecake

Serve this easy-to-prepare dessert at your next party. . . look for compliments.

Crust:
1½ cups graham cracker crumbs
¼ cup granulated sugar
5 tablespoons butter, melted and cooled

Topping:
1½ cups chopped pecans
½ cup brown sugar, packed
2 tablespoons water

Filling:
1 8-ounce package cream
  cheese, softened
½ cup brown sugar, packed
1 teaspoon cinnamon
½ cup cornstarch
2 large eggs
1 teaspoon pure vanilla extract
1 30-ounce can pumpkin pie mix

Preheat oven to 350°.

Crust: Stir together all crust ingredients in a small bowl; press mixture onto bottom and 1 inch up sides of a 9-inch springform baking pan.

Topping: Stir together all topping ingredients in a small bowl; reserve 1 cup of topping. Sprinkle remaining mixture over crumbs in baking pan.

Filling: Beat cream cheese, brown sugar, cinnamon and cornstarch in a medium bowl with an electric mixer until creamy. Beat in eggs and vanilla until blended. Beat in pumpkin pie mix. Spoon mixture over pecan mixture in baking pan.

Bake 50–60 minutes or until center is almost set. Sprinkle with reserved topping. Bake until center is set, about 10 minutes. Remove from oven. Run a thin knife around edge of cheesecake. Cool in pan. Chill, then remove side of pan. Store in the refrigerator.

Makes 16 servings.

One serving contains approximately: Calories 340, Fat 18g, Carbohydrates 41g, Protein 4g

Pumpkin Cheesecake

This is a great dessert for the holidays. Top with whipped cream when serving.

Crust:
1½ cups graham cracker crumbs
3 tablespoons granulated sugar
5 tablespoons butter,
    melted and cooled

Filling:
3 8-ounce packages cream
    cheese, softened
1 cup granulated sugar
3 eggs
1 cup canned pumpkin (not pie mix)
1½ teaspoons pure vanilla extract
1 teaspoon ground cinnamon
¼ teaspoon ground nutmeg
¼ teaspoon ground ginger
⅛ teaspoon ground cloves

Preheat oven to 350°. Grease a 9-inch springform baking pan.

Crust: Mix all crust ingredients in a small bowl. Press mixture onto bottom and 2 inches up sides of pan. Bake 5 minutes. Cool on a wire rack; set aside.

Filling: Beat cream cheese and 1 cup granulated sugar in a large mixer bowl on medium speed until smooth. Beat in eggs, one at a time. Beat in remaining filling ingredients until just blended. Pour mixture into baked crust.

Bake about 1 hour and 20 minutes or until center is almost set. Cool in pan 10 minutes on a wire rack. Run a thin knife around edge to loosen cake from pan. Cool in pan 1 hour on a wire rack, then immediately refrigerate and cool completely. Remove side of pan just before serving. Store in the refrigerator.

Makes 12 servings.

Variation: Use crushed gingersnap cookie to make the crumb crust.

One serving contains approximately: Calories 245, Fat 14g, Carbohydrates 28g, Protein 4g

Pumpkin Cheesecake Cups

Top each serving with a dollop of sweetened whipped cream.

⅔ cup crushed gingersnap cookies
2 tablespoons butter, melted
  and cooled

1 8-ounce package cream
  cheese, softened
½ cup granulated sugar

1 cup canned pumpkin (not pie mix)
1 teaspoon pumpkin pie spice
1 teaspoon pure vanilla extract
2 large eggs

Preheat oven to 325°. Line 12 muffin cups with paper muffin liners.

Mix together cookie crumbs and butter in a small bowl. Press equal amounts onto the bottom of each muffin cup. Bake 4 minutes. Remove from oven; set aside.

Beat cream cheese and sugar in a small mixer bowl with an electric mixer until creamy. Add pumpkin, pumpkin pie spice and vanilla; beat until blended. Add eggs; beat well. Spoon batter equally into cups, filling each three-quarters full.

Bake 25–30 minutes. Cool in pan on a wire rack. Remove cups from pan and refrigerate. Serve chilled. Refrigerate leftovers.

Makes 12 servings.

One serving contains approximately: Calories 170, Fat 11g, Carbohydrates 16g, Protein 3g

Winter Squash Cheesecake Bars

Variation: Use regular cream cheese instead of reduced-fat cream cheese.

Crust:
½ cup uncooked old-fashioned oats
10 full-size graham crackers
2 tablespoons granulated sugar
¼ cup all-purpose flour
2 tablespoons butter
3 tablespoons milk

Filling:
2 8-ounce packages reduced-fat
    cream cheese, softened
½ cup granulated sugar
2 large eggs
½ cup winter squash puree
1 teaspoon pure vanilla extract
½ teaspoon ground cinnamon
¼ teaspoon ground nutmeg
¼ teaspoon salt
3 tablespoons all-purpose flour

Preheat oven to 350°. Grease a 13x9-inch baking pan.

Crust: Place oats, graham crackers, 2 tablespoons sugar, ¼ cup flour and butter in a food processor; process until finely ground. Add milk; pulse to moisten. Pat mixture into bottom of prepared baking pan. Bake 10 minutes. Cool on a wire rack; set aside.

Filling: Reduce heat to 325°. Beat cream cheese and ½ cup sugar in a large mixer bowl with an electric mixer until creamy. Beat in eggs one at a time. Beat in squash puree, vanilla extract, cinnamon, nutmeg, salt and 3 tablespoons flour. Spread mixture over crust baking pan.

Bake about 35 minutes or until set. Cool completely in pan on a wire rack, then immediately refrigerate. Chill before cutting. Store in the refrigerator.

Makes 18 bars.

One serving contains approximately: Calories 148, Fat 6g, Carbohydrates 18g, Protein 5g

Pies

Apple and Fresh Pumpkin Pie

You'll find apple and pumpkin in this good pie. Serve warm or at room temperature topped with a scoop of vanilla or cinnamon ice cream.

⅓ cup light brown sugar, packed
1 tablespoon cornstarch
1 teaspoon ground cinnamon, divided
½ teaspoon salt, divided
⅓ cup cold water
2 tablespoons butter
3 cups thinly sliced Granny
  Smith apples
1 9-inch unbaked pie crust
  (in pie pan)

1 egg
⅓ cup granulated sugar
¾ cup freshly cooked
  pumpkin puree
¼ teaspoon ground cloves
¼ teaspoon ground ginger
¾ cup evaporated milk
1 teaspoon pure vanilla extract

Preheat oven to 425°.

Place brown sugar, cornstarch, ½ teaspoon ground cinnamon, ¼ teaspoon salt, water and butter into a medium saucepan. Cook over medium heat, stirring constantly, until mixture comes to a boil. Add apples; toss to coat and cook an additional about 4 minutes. Pour mixture into pie crust.

In a large bowl, whisk together egg, granulated sugar, pumpkin, ½ teaspoon cinnamon, ¼ teaspoon salt, cloves, ginger, milk and vanilla extract. Spoon mixture over apple mixture in pie crust. Bake 10 minutes, then reduce heat to 375°. Bake until filling is just set in the middle, about 40 minutes more. Cool completely in pan on a wire rack. Cut into slices. Serve. Refrigerate leftovers.

Makes 8 servings.

One serving contains approximately: Calories 220, Fat 9g, Carbohydrates 33g, Protein 3g

Butternut Squash Pie

Top with sweetened whipped cream when serving.

Crust:
½ cup butter, softened
⅓ cup brown sugar, packed
1¼ cups all-purpose flour
½ cup chopped pecans
½ teaspoon pure vanilla extract
¼ teaspoon salt
¼ teaspoon baking soda

Filling:
2 eggs
1 cup cooked mashed butternut squash
¾ cup brown sugar, packed
1 teaspoon ground cinnamon
¼ teaspoon each: ground ginger, ground cloves, ground nutmeg
½ teaspoon salt
1 teaspoon pure vanilla extract
1 12-ounce can evaporated milk

Preheat oven to 425°.

Crust: In a large bowl, mix together butter and ⅓ cup brown sugar. Stir in all remaining crust ingredients until crumbly. Press mixture onto bottom and up sides of a deep-dish pie plate (9x1½ inches); flute edges ½-inch high to keep filling from running over.

Filling: In a large bowl, beat eggs slightly. Stir in squash, ¾ cup brown sugar, cinnamon, ginger, cloves, nutmeg, salt and 1 teaspoon vanilla extract. Gradually stir in evaporated milk until mixture is smooth. Pour mixture into pie crust.

Bake 15 minutes, then reduce heat to 350°. (Cover edge of crust with aluminum foil strips to avoid excessive browning.) Continue baking 45–55 minutes or until knife inserted in center comes out clean. Cool on wire rack. Store in refrigerator.

Makes 8 servings.

Variation: Use pumpkin instead of squash.

One serving contains approximately: Calories 400, Fat 19g, Carbohydrates 53g, Protein 5g

Creamy Two-Layer Pumpkin Pie

Serve chilled pie with a dollop of sweetened cinnamon whipped cream.

2 8-ounce packages cream cheese, softened
½ cup granulated sugar
2 eggs
1 teaspoon pure vanilla extract
½ cup canned pumpkin (not pie mix)
½ teaspoon ground cinnamon
¼ teaspoon ground nutmeg
⅛ teaspoon ground cloves

1 6-ounce purchased graham cracker pie crust, or homemade

Preheat oven to 325°.

In a large mixer bowl, beat cream cheese and sugar with an electric mixer until smooth. Beat in eggs and vanilla. Remove 1 cup batter and place in a small bowl; stir in pumpkin and spices. Pour remaining plain batter into pie crust. Top evenly with pumpkin batter.

Bake about 40 minutes or until center is almost set. Cool slightly on a wire rack, then immediately refrigerate. Chill for at least three hours before serving. Refrigerate leftovers.

Makes 8 servings.

One serving contains approximately: Calories 380, Fat 26g, Carbohydrates 29g, Protein 6g

Fresh Sugar Pumpkin Pie

This is a good way to use fresh pie pumpkins. Serve plain or with whipped cream.

Crust:
1 unbaked 10-inch
   deep-dish pie crust

Filling:
2 cups freshly cooked sugar
   pumpkin, mashed
¾ cup granulated sugar
¼ teaspoon salt
1¼ teaspoons ground cinnamon
1 teaspoon ground ginger
½ teaspoon ground nutmeg
¼ teaspoon ground cloves

3 large eggs
1 12-ounce can evaporated milk
½ cup whole milk
1 teaspoon pure vanilla extract

Preheat oven to 400°. Line a 10-inch deep-dish pie pan with unbaked crust; flute the edges.

In large bowl, mix together, pumpkin, granulated sugar, salt and spices; set aside.

In a medium bowl, beat eggs lightly. Add evaporated milk, whole milk and vanilla; beat until blended. Add to pumpkin mixture; mix well (filling will be thin). Pour into unbaked pie crust until almost full (be careful not to overfill; discard any extra).

Bake about 50–60 minutes or until a knife inserted in center comes out clean. Cool completely on a wire rack. Chill before serving. Store in the refrigerator.

Makes 8 servings.

One serving contains approximately: Calories 268, Fat 10g, Carbohydrates 30g, Protein 8g

Mary's Little Pumpkin Pies

Serve this easy dessert in place of regular pie.

1 cup canned pumpkin puree (not pie mix)
½ cup baking mix, such as Bisquick
½ cup granulated sugar
¾ teaspoon ground cinnamon
½ teaspoon ground ginger
¼ teaspoon ground cloves
¾ cup evaporated milk
1 teaspoon pure vanilla extract
2 eggs, slightly beaten

1 cup non-dairy whipped topping

Preheat oven to 375°. Spray 12 regular-size muffin cups with cooking spray.

In a large bowl, mix all ingredients except thawed whipped topping until blended.
Place ¼ cup mixture into each cup.

Bake about 30 minutes or until edges start pulling away from sides of cups.
Remove from oven; cool 10 minutes, then loosen sides of pies with a thin knife.
Remove pies from cups; place on a wire rack. Cool slightly before serving.
Top each pie with a tablespoon whipped topping. Refrigerate leftovers.

Makes 12 servings.

One serving contains approximately: Calories 90 Fat 2g Carbohydrates 15g Protein 2g

Mini Whoopie Pumpkin Pies

These sweet treats will disappear fast when the kids are around.

2 cups all-purpose flour
1 teaspoon baking powder
1 teaspoon baking soda
1 teaspoon ground cinnamon
½ teaspoon ground ginger
½ teaspoon salt

½ cup butter, softened
1¼ cups granulated sugar

2 large eggs
1 cup canned pumpkin (not pie mix)
1 teaspoon pure vanilla extract

Filling:
4 ounces cream cheese, softened
6 tablespoons butter, softened
½ teaspoon pure vanilla extract
1½ cups powdered sugar

Preheat oven to 350°. Lightly grease 4 baking sheets.

Mix flour, baking powder, soda, cinnamon, ginger and salt in a medium bowl; set aside.

In a large bowl, beat butter and granulated sugar on medium speed until smooth. Beat in eggs, one at a time. Beat in pumpkin and 1 teaspoon vanilla until blended. Stir in flour mixture until combined. Drop dough by the heaping teaspoonful onto prepared baking sheets. Bake about 10–12 minutes or until cookie springs back when touched. Cool on baking sheets 5 minutes. Remove cookies and cool completely on a wire rack.

Filling: Beat cream cheese, butter and ½ teaspoon vanilla in a small bowl until fluffy. On low speed, gradually beat in powdered sugar until blended. Spread a heaping teaspoonful on the flat side of one cookie. Top with the flat side of second cookie; press down gently. Repeat with remaining cookies and filling. Refrigerate.

Makes 36 servings.

One serving contains approximately: Calories 130, Fat 6g, Carbohydrates 18g, Protein 1g

Pumpkin Chiffon Pie

Chiffon pie is a perfect dessert to serve for special occasions.

Crust:
1¾ cups finely ground gingersnap
   cookie crumbs
2 tablespoons granulated sugar
⅓ cup melted butter

Filling:
2 envelopes unflavored gelatin
¼ cup boiling water
1 5-ounce can evaporated milk

1 30-ounce can pumpkin pie mix
1 teaspoon pure vanilla extract
1 3-ounce box vanilla instant pudding
   and pie filling mix
1 teaspoon pumpkin pie spice
1½ cups thawed non-dairy
   whipped topping

Preheat oven to 350°. Grease a deep-dish pie plate.

Crust: Mix all crust ingredients in a small bowl; reserve ⅓ cup mixture. Press remaining mixture on bottom and up sides of prepared pie plate. Bake 8 minutes. Remove from oven; cool completely on a wire rack.

Filling: Place gelatin in a small saucepan. Pour boiling water over gelatin; let stand 1 minute. Heat gelatin over low heat until dissolved. Add evaporated milk, stirring constantly until just hot but not boiling. Remove from heat; set aside.

In a large mixer bowl, beat pumpkin, vanilla, pudding mix, pie spice and gelatin mixture on high speed 3 minutes. Gently fold in whipped topping. Spoon mixture into crust. Sprinkle with ⅓ cup reserved crumb mixture. Immediately refrigerate. Chill 2 hours or until firm enough to cut. Refrigerate leftovers.

Makes 8 servings.

One serving contains approximately: Calories 370, Fat 14g, Carbohydrates 57g, Protein 5g

Pumpkin Cream Cheese Pie

Serve this delicious pie with dollops of sweetened whipped cream

1 9-inch refrigerated pie crust

11 ounces cream cheese, softened
   (1 8-ounce package plus 1 3-ounce package)
1 cup granulated sugar
3 tablespoons all-purpose flour
1½ teaspoons pumpkin spice
3 eggs
1 teaspoon pure vanilla extract
1 15-ounce can pumpkin (not pie mix)

Preheat oven to 375°.

Place pie crust in a 9-inch glass pie plate following the package directions for a one-crust filled pie. Bake until light brown, about 8 minutes. Remove from oven; set aside.

In a large mixing bowl, beat cream cheese and sugar with an electric mixer until smooth. Add remaining ingredients; beat until blended. Pour mixture into crust.

Bake 35–45 minutes or until a knife inserted in the center comes out clean. Cool 30 minutes, then cover and refrigerate. Chill 2 hours before serving. Store in the refrigerator.

Makes 8 servings.

One serving contains approximately: Calories 380, Fat 21g, Carbohydrates 41g, Protein 7g

Pumpkin Cream Pie

Serve this creamy pumpkin pie for a holiday dessert.

Crust:
1 9-inch refrigerated unbaked
    pie crust

First Layer:
⅓ cup granulated sugar
1 8-ounce package cream
    cheese, softened
1 teaspoon pure vanilla extract
¼ teaspoon ground cardamom
1 egg

Pumpkin Layer:
¾ cup brown sugar, packed
2 eggs, beaten
1 15-ounce can pumpkin (not pie mix)
1 tablespoon all-purpose flour
1½ teaspoons pumpkin pie spice
½ cup half-and-half

Topping:
1 cup whipping cream
2 tablespoons granulated sugar
½ teaspoon pure vanilla extract

Preheat oven to 375°.
Crust: Prepare crust following package directions for unbaked 9-inch one-crust pie.

First Layer: Beat granulated sugar, cream cheese, vanilla and cardamom in a medium bowl on medium speed until fluffy. Beat in 1 egg. Spread mixture into crust.

Pumpkin Layer: In a large bowl, stir together all pumpkin layer ingredients except half-and-half until blended. Gradually stir in half-and-half. Spoon carefully over first layer in crust. Cover edges of crust with strips of aluminum foil. Bake 30 minutes. Remove foil; continue baking 30–40 minutes or until a knife inserted in center comes out clean. Cool on a wire rack 2 hours, then refrigerate well before serving.

Topping: Beat cream, sugar and vanilla on high speed in a medium bowl until stiff peaks form. Spread whipped cream on chilled pie. Serve. Refrigerate leftovers.

Makes 8 servings.

One serving contains approximately: Calories 470, Fat 28g, Carbohydrates 50g, Protein 8g

Pumpkin Ice Cream Pie

If you like ice cream, you will love this pie! Top with sweetened whipped cream.

Crust:
1½ cups graham cracker crumbs
3 tablespoons granulated sugar
6 tablespoons butter, melted and cooled

Filling:
1 cup canned pumpkin puree (not pie mix)
½ cup brown sugar, packed
½ teaspoon salt, scant
½ teaspoon ground ginger
½ teaspoon ground cinnamon
½ teaspoon ground nutmeg

1 quart vanilla ice cream
¼ cup toasted pecans, finely chopped

Crust: In a small bowl, mix all crust ingredients until blended. Press mixture onto bottom of a lightly buttered 9-inch deep-dish pie plate. Freeze.

Filling: In a medium bowl, stir together all filling ingredients except ice cream and pecans until well mixed; set aside.

In a large bowl, gently stir ice cream to soften, then quickly fold in pumpkin mixture until blended. Pour mixture into prepared crust. Sprinkle pecans in a circle around outer edge of filling. Freeze until firm. Cover with aluminum foil when frozen and return to freezer. Remove from freezer 10 minutes before serving. Freeze leftovers.

Makes 8 servings.

One serving contains approximately: Calories 468, Fat 22g, Carbohydrates 65g, Protein 5g

Tofu-Pumpkin-Pecan Pie

Tofu makes this pie silky smooth. Serve with thawed frozen non-dairy topping.

Crust:
1¼ cups all-purpose flour
¼ cup pecan pieces
½ teaspoon salt
1 tablespoon granulated sugar
½ cup vegetable shortening
2 to 3 tablespoons ice water

¾ cup pecan halves, mixed with
   2 tablespoons maple syrup
   in a bowl

Filling:
1 16-ounce package extra-firm
   silken tofu, drained
1 15-ounce can pumpkin puree
   (not pie mix)
½ cup granulated sugar
¼ cup maple syrup
1 teaspoon pure vanilla extract
½ teaspoon salt
1 teaspoon ground cinnamon
½ teaspoon ground ginger
¼ teaspoon ground cloves

Crust: In a food processor, pulse flour, pecans, salt and 1 tablespoon granulated sugar until pecans are finely ground. Add shortening; pulse until almost combined. Add ice water; pulse until just blended. Form dough into a ball then press into a flat disk and wrap in plastic wrap; chill. Take dough out and let stand 15 minutes. Roll dough out on a floured surface into an 11-inch circle; place in a 9-inch pie plate. Adjust to fit. Crimp edges. Place pecan halves in bottom of pie shell.

Filling: In a food processor, process tofu until smooth. Add remaining filling ingredients; puree until smooth. Pour into pie shell.

Preheat oven to 400°.

Bake about 1 hour or until a knife inserted in the center comes out clean. Cool on a wire rack. Slice and serve. Refrigerate leftovers.

Makes 12 servings.

One serving contains approximately: Calories 420, Fat 27g, Carbohydrates 42g, Protein 7g

Turtle Pumpkin Pie

This pie is sure to become a favorite . . . so easy to prepare.

1 6-ounce graham cracker pie crust, purchased or homemade
¼ cup plus 2 tablespoons caramel ice cream topping, divided
½ cup plus 2 tablespoons chopped toasted pecans, divided

1 cup cold whole milk
2 3.4-ounce packages vanilla flavor instant pudding mix
1 cup canned pumpkin (not pie mix)
1 teaspoon ground cinnamon
½ teaspoon ground nutmeg
⅛ teaspoon ground ginger
1 teaspoon pure vanilla extract

1 8-ounce container frozen non-dairy whipped topping, thawed, divided

Pour ¼ cup caramel topping into pie crust then sprinkle with ½ cup pecans.

Beat milk, pudding mix, pumpkin, cinnamon, nutmeg, ginger and vanilla extract in a large bowl on low speed until blended. Stir in 1½ cups whipped topping. Spoon mixture into pie crust and immediately refrigerate. Chill 1 hour before serving.

Top pie with remaining whipped topping, caramel topping and pecans when serving. Store in the refrigerator.

Makes 10 servings.

One serving contains approximately: Calories 320, Fat 15g, Carbohydrates 48g, Protein 3g

Zucchini Pie

This tastes like apple pie . . . serve warm with vanilla ice cream.

2 9-inch unbaked pie crusts

¾ cup granulated sugar
2 tablespoons cornstarch
2 tablespoons tapioca
½ teaspoon salt
2 teaspoons ground cinnamon
½ teaspoon ground nutmeg

4 cups thinly sliced fresh zucchini
¼ cup fresh lemon juice
1 teaspoon pure vanilla extract

2 tablespoons cold butter,
  cut into small pieces
1 tablespoon whole milk
½ teaspoon granulated sugar

Preheat oven to 400°. Line a 9-inch pie pan with one unbaked crust.

In a large bowl, mix together ¾ cup sugar, cornstarch, tapioca, salt, cinnamon and nutmeg until well blended.

Add zucchini, lemon juice and vanilla extract; mix well. Pour mixture into pie crust. Dot with butter. Top with second crust; crimp edges together and flute. Cut 3 slits in top crust to vent steam. Brush top with milk then sprinkle with ½ teaspoon sugar. Bake 15 minutes, then reduce heat to 350° and continue baking for about 50 minutes. Cool on a wire rack. Serve. Refrigerate leftovers.

Makes 8 servings.

Variation: Make a lattice crust for the top of the pie.

One serving contains approximately: Calories 335, Fat 17g, Carbohydrates 46g, Protein 3g

Desserts

Cake Mix Pumpkin Pie Dessert

Serve this easy dessert with sweetened whipped cream.

Crust:
1 18.25-ounce spice cake mix, divided
½ cup butter, melted
1 large egg

Filling:
⅔ cup whole milk
1 30-ounce can pumpkin pie mix
2 eggs
1 teaspoon pure vanilla extract

Topping:
1 cup reserved cake mix
¼ cup brown sugar, packed
¼ cup butter, softened
½ cup chopped pecans

Preheat oven to 350°. Grease a 13x9-inch baking pan.

Reserve 1 cup of cake mix.

Crust: In a large bowl, beat remaining cake mix, melted butter and 1 egg, using an electric mixer on low speed, until well mixed. Spread batter in bottom of prepared baking pan; set aside.

Filling: In same bowl, beat all filling ingredients until smooth; pour filling over crust.

Topping: In a medium bowl, mix reserved 1 cup cake mix, brown sugar and ¼ cup butter until coarse crumbs form. Stir in pecans; sprinkle mixture over filling.

Bake 50–60 minutes or until a knife inserted in center comes out clean. Cool in pan 15 minutes. Cut into squares. Serve warm or cool. Store in the refrigerator.

Makes 15 servings.

One serving contains approximately: Calories 320, Fat 17g, Carbohydrates 42g, Protein 4g

Country Pumpkin Custard

Custard is a favorite of old and young alike. Serve this treat topped with sweetened whipped cream.

Filling:
1 15-ounce can pumpkin (not pie mix)
2 eggs, slightly beaten
1 cup half-and-half
1 teaspoon pure vanilla extract
⅔ cup brown sugar, packed
1½ teaspoons pumpkin pie spice
½ teaspoon salt

Topping:
¼ cup brown sugar, packed
¼ cup chopped pecans
1 tablespoon butter, melted

Preheat oven to 350°. Grease four 10-ounce custard baking cups.

Filling: In a large bowl, mix pumpkin, eggs, half-and-half, vanilla extract, ⅔ cup brown sugar, pumpkin pie spice and salt until well blended. Pour mixture equally into prepared baking cups. Place cups in a 13x9-inch baking pan; pour hot water around cups to a 1-inch depth. Bake uncovered 20 minutes.

Topping: In a small bowl, mix together ¼ cup brown sugar, pecans and melted butter. Sprinkle mixture equally over filling in cups, and continue baking about 35 minutes longer or until a knife inserted in the center comes out clean. Cool slightly on a wire rack. Serve warm or cool. Store in the refrigerator.

Makes 4 servings.

One serving contains approximately: Calories 422, Fat 17g, Carbohydrates 61g, Protein 8g

Ice Cream Pumpkin Squares

Hard to resist this dessert . . . top with whipped cream and toasted chopped pecans.

1¼ cups graham cracker crumbs
¼ cup butter, softened
1 tablespoon granulated sugar

1 cup canned pumpkin (not pie mix)
½ cup brown sugar, packed
½ teaspoon ground cinnamon
½ teaspoon ground ginger
¼ teaspoon ground nutmeg

1 quart vanilla ice cream (4 cups), softened

Mix graham cracker crumbs, butter and granulated sugar in a small bowl; press mixture evenly and firmly onto bottom of an 8- or 9-inch-square baking pan.

In a large bowl, stir together pumpkin, brown sugar and spices. Stir in softened ice cream with a spoon; spread over crumb crust in pan. Freeze uncovered until firm. Cover and store in the freezer. Remove from freezer 10 minutes before cutting. Freeze leftovers.

Makes 9 servings.

One serving contains approximately: Calories 290, Fat 13g, Carbohydrates 38g, Protein 2g

No-Cook Pumpkin Pudding

Top each serving with finely crushed gingersnap cookie crumbs for extra goodness.

1½ cups cold whole milk
1 cup whipping cream, divided
1 3.4-ounce package instant pudding mix
¾ teaspoon ground cinnamon
¼ teaspoon ground ginger
¼ teaspoon ground cloves
1 cup canned pumpkin (not pie mix)
1 teaspoon pure vanilla extract, divided
1 tablespoon granulated sugar

In a medium bowl, whisk together milk, ½ cup whipping cream, pudding mix and spices until thickened and smooth, about 3 minutes. Stir in pumpkin and ½ teaspoon vanilla extract until blended. Spoon pudding into 4 dessert dishes.

Add ½ cup whipping cream, ½ teaspoon vanilla and granulated sugar to small bowl; whip until stiff peaks form. Spoon equal dollops onto each pudding.

Serve or immediately refrigerate. Refrigerate leftovers.

Makes 4 servings.

One serving contains approximately: Calories 250, Fat 17g, Carbohydrates 22g, Protein 4g

Pumpkin Bread Pudding

Fresh pumpkin puree is used in this bread pudding. Serve warm or at room temperature with whipped cream or vanilla ice cream.

5 cups freshly cooked pumpkin puree
2 whole eggs
2 egg yolks
3 cups half-and-half
1 teaspoon pure vanilla extract
¼ cup dark brown sugar, packed
1¼ cups granulated sugar, divided
¾ teaspoon ground cinnamon

¼ teaspoon ground nutmeg
¼ teaspoon ground cardamom, optional

2 tablespoons cold water
1 cup heavy whipping cream, divided
10 cups 2-inch cubes challah bread or Italian bread

In a large bowl, mix pumpkin, whole eggs, egg yolks, half-and-half, vanilla extract, brown sugar, ¼ cup granulated sugar, cinnamon, nutmeg and cardamom; set aside.

In a small saucepan mix 2 tablespoons cold water and 1 cup granulated sugar. Heat over high heat. As sugar melts, swirl pan often for even melting (do not stir with a spoon). Cook until sugar has a deep caramel color, about 3 to 4 minutes. Remove from heat.

Carefully whisk ¼ cup whipping cream into caramel until combined, then whisk in remaining ¾ cup whipping cream. Pour mixture into a 2½-quart baking dish.

Top with half the bread cubes, then pour half the pumpkin mixture over the top. Top with remaining bread, then with remaining pumpkin mixture. Let sit 30 minutes.

Preheat oven to 350°.
Bake until set, about 35–45 minutes. Serve. Refrigerate leftovers.

Makes 15 servings.

One serving contains approximately: Calories 340, Fat 14g, Carbohydrates 47g, Protein 8g

Pumpkin-Cookie Ice Cream

Homemade pumpkin is used in this ice cream.

1 pint heavy whipping cream
½ cup whole milk
1 cup light brown sugar, packed
1 cup homemade pumpkin puree
1 teaspoon ground cinnamon
¾ teaspoon ground ginger
¼ teaspoon salt
2 teaspoons pure vanilla extract

½ cup coarsely broken gingersnaps cookies

In a large bowl, mix together all ingredients except gingersnap cookies. Strain mixture into an ice cream maker; freeze following manufacturer's directions.

Place ice cream in a medium bowl; stir in gingersnap cookies. Spoon mixture into a clean plastic food container; cover and freeze until ready to serve, about 3 hours. Store covered in the freezer. Makes about 1 quart.

Makes 8 servings.

One serving contains approximately: Calories 371, Fat 24g, Carbohydrates 39g, Protein 2g

Pumpkin Cream Cheese Parfaits

This delicious dessert requires no cooking!

1 8-ounce package Neufchatel cream cheese
1 cup canned pumpkin (not pie mix)
5 tablespoons pure maple syrup, divided
6 tablespoons honey
¾ teaspoon ground cinnamon, divided
⅛ teaspoon ground nutmeg
1 cup whipping cream
½ teaspoon pure vanilla extract
½ cup chopped pecans

Beat cream cheese in a medium bowl until smooth. Add pumpkin, 3 tablespoons syrup, honey, ½ teaspoon cinnamon and nutmeg; beat on low speed until blended.

Beat whipping cream with an electric beater in a medium bowl until soft peaks form. Add vanilla extract, 2 tablespoons syrup and ¼ teaspoon cinnamon; beat until stiff peaks form.

Spoon half of the pumpkin mixture evenly into 6 parfait glasses. Top evenly with half of the whipped cream and half of the pecans. Repeat layers. Chill. Serve. Refrigerate leftovers.

Makes 6 servings.

One serving contains approximately: Calories 400, Fat 28g, Carbohydrates 36g, Protein 6g

Pumpkin Cream Cheese Roll

This delicious dessert is the perfect holiday treat for special guests.

3 eggs
1 cup granulated sugar
⅔ cup canned pumpkin
   (not pie mix)
¾ cup all-purpose flour
1 teaspoon baking soda
1 teaspoon ground cinnamon
½ teaspoon ground ginger

¼ teaspoon ground nutmeg
½ cup finely chopped walnuts, optional
⅓ cup butter, softened
2 3-ounce packages cream
   cheese, softened
1 teaspoon pure vanilla extract
1½ cups powdered sugar
½ teaspoon ground ginger

Preheat oven to 350°.
Spray a 15x10x1-inch jelly roll baking pan with nonstick cooking spray. Then line the bottom of the pan with parchment paper. Spray parchment paper with nonstick cooking spray; set aside. Place a clean kitchen towel flat on kitchen counter and generously sprinkle lightly all over with powdered sugar; set aside.

Beat eggs in a large mixer bowl with an electric mixer on high until light and foamy. Beat in granulated sugar until well mixed. Beat in pumpkin. Mix flour, baking soda, cinnamon, ½ teaspoon ginger and nutmeg in a bowl; gradually beat into pumpkin mixture on low until well mixed. Stir in walnuts. Spread batter into prepared pan. Bake 14 minutes or until cake springs back when lightly touched. Immediately invert cake onto prepared towel. Lift off pan; carefully peel off parchment paper. Starting at 10-inch side, carefully roll up cake in towel. Cool completely.

Beat butter and cream cheese in a large bowl until creamy. Add remaining ingredients; beat on low until blended. Unroll cake and spread filling to within ½ inch of edges. Starting at 10-inch side, roll up cake. Wrap in plastic wrap. Chill. Sprinkle with powdered sugar just before serving. Cut into slices. Serve. Refrigerate.

Makes 12 servings.

One serving contains approximately: Calories 300, Fat 15g, Carbohydrates 40g, Protein 4g

Pumpkin Crisp

A cake mix is used in this delicious crisp. Serve with vanilla ice cream.

1 18.25-ounce package yellow
  cake mix, divided
1 egg
½ cup butter, melted

¼ teaspoon ground ginger
½ cup granulated sugar
⅔ cup evaporated milk
1 teaspoon pure vanilla extract

1 29-ounce can pumpkin puree
  (not pie mix)
2 eggs
1 teaspoon ground cinnamon
½ teaspoon ground nutmeg

½ cup granulated sugar
½ cup butter, softened

Preheat oven to 350°. Lightly butter a 13x9-inch baking pan.

Reserve 1 cup cake mix.

In a medium bowl, mix together remaining cake mix, 1 egg and ½ cup butter until crumbly; pat mixture into prepared baking pan.

In a large bowl, mix together pumpkin, 2 eggs, spices, ½ cup granulated sugar, milk and vanilla; pour mixture over crust in pan.

In a medium bowl, mix 1 cup reserved cake mix, ½ cup granulated sugar and ½ cup butter until coarse crumbs form; sprinkle evenly over pumpkin mixture.

Bake 55–60 minutes. Serve warm. Refrigerate leftovers.

Makes 18 servings.

One serving contains approximately: Calories 298, Fat 15g, Carbohydrates 40g, Protein 3g

Pretzel-Crusted Pumpkin Cheesecake Dessert

Only the crust is baked in this creamy pumpkin dessert.

1 6-ounce bag pretzel crisps, crushed into fine crumbs
6 tablespoons butter, melted
1 cup light brown sugar, divided

2 cups pumpkin puree (not pie mix)
2 8-ounce packages Neufchatel cream cheese

1 tablespoon pure vanilla extract
1¾ teaspoons ground cinnamon, divided
½ teaspoon ground cloves

½ cup heavy whipping cream
½ cup toasted pecans, finely chopped

Preheat oven to 350°. Butter a 13x9-inch glass baking dish.

Mix crumbs, butter and 2 tablespoons brown sugar in a medium bowl; press mixture firmly into prepared dish. Bake 10 minutes. Remove from oven; cool.

Beat pumpkin, cream cheese, ¾ cup brown sugar, vanilla extract, 1½ teaspoons cinnamon and cloves in a large mixer bowl with an electric mixer until smooth and creamy. Pour mixture over completely cooled crust.

Beat cream and 2 tablespoons brown sugar in a large bowl until stiff peaks form; drop by the tablespoonful onto pumpkin mixture; carefully swirl the two mixtures together with a thin spatula. Sprinkle evenly with pecans. Sprinkle with ¼ teaspoon cinnamon. Cover and chill at least 8 hours before serving. Refrigerate leftovers.

Makes 12 servings.

Variation: Use regular cream cheese.

One serving contains approximately: Calories 350, Fat 21g, Carbohydrates, 34g, Protein 5g

Spicy Pumpkin Dessert Squares

Top each serving with whipped cream as desired.

Filling:
1 cup brown sugar, packed
¼ cup granulated sugar
1 29-ounce can pumpkin puree
  (not pie mix)
1 12-ounce can evaporated milk
5 eggs
1 teaspoon pure vanilla extract
2 teaspoons ground cinnamon
½ teaspoon ground ginger
½ teaspoon ground cloves

Topping:
¾ cup all-purpose flour
½ cup brown sugar, packed
¼ cup cold butter, cut into
  small pieces
½ cup chopped pecans

Preheat oven to 350°. Grease a 13x9-inch baking dish.

Filling: In a large bowl, beat all filling ingredients until smooth. Pour mixture into prepared baking dish. Bake 20–25 minutes or until partially set.

Topping: In a small bowl, mix flour, ½ cup brown sugar and butter with a pastry blender or fork until coarse crumbs form. Stir in pecans; sprinkle mixture over hot partially baked pumpkin filling and continue baking 15–20 minutes or until a knife inserted in the center comes out clean. Cool in baking dish for 30 minutes, then refrigerate and cool completely. Cut into squares. Store in the refrigerator.

Makes 15 servings.

One serving contains approximately: Calories 250, Fat 9g, Carbohydrates 37g, Protein 5g

Zucchini Cobbler

Serve this tasty cobbler with whipped topping or vanilla ice cream.

Filling:
8 cups peeled and seeded fresh zucchini
⅔ cup fresh lemon juice
1 cup granulated sugar
1 teaspoon ground cinnamon
½ teaspoon ground nutmeg
1 teaspoon pure vanilla extract

Crust:
4 cups all-purpose flour
2 cups granulated sugar
1½ cups cold butter, cut into
   small pieces

1 teaspoon ground cinnamon

Preheat oven to 375°. Grease a 15x10x1-inch baking pan.

Filling: Place zucchini and lemon juice in a large saucepan. Cook and stir over medium heat until tender, about 10 minutes. Stir in 1 cup sugar, 1 teaspoon cinnamon and nutmeg; simmer mixture 1 minute. Remove from heat; stir in vanilla extract. Set aside.

Crust: Mix together flour and 2 cups sugar in a large bowl. Cut in butter with a pastry blender until coarse crumbs are formed. Stir ½ cup of the crust mixture into the zucchini mixture.

Press half of remaining crust mixture into prepared baking pan. Spoon zucchini mixture over the top. Crumble remaining crust mixture over zucchini mixture. Sprinkle with 1 teaspoon ground cinnamon.

Bake about 35–40 minutes, until golden and bubbly. Serve. Refrigerate leftovers.

Makes 16 servings.

One serving contains approximately: Calories 340, Fat 14g, Carbohydrates 51g, Protein 3g

Zucchini Crisp

Top each serving with a scoop of vanilla ice cream.

Filling:
8 cups peeled fresh zucchini, cut
  diagonally into ¾-inch slices
¾ cup fresh lemon juice
½ cup granulated sugar
2 teaspoons ground cinnamon
½ teaspoon ground nutmeg
1 teaspoon pure vanilla extract

Topping:
1⅓ cups brown sugar
1 cup all-purpose flour
1 cup uncooked quick oats
½ teaspoon salt
⅔ cup butter, softened

Preheat oven to 375°. Grease a 13x9-inch baking pan.

Filling: Cook zucchini and lemon juice in a large saucepan over medium heat, stirring occasionally, until tender. Stir in granulated sugar, cinnamon and nutmeg until sugar is dissolved. Remove from heat; stir in vanilla extract. Pour mixture into prepared pan.

Topping: Mix together brown sugar, flour, oats, salt and butter in a medium bowl until crumbly.

Sprinkle mixture over zucchini mixture. Bake about 45–50 minutes or until topping is golden brown. Serve warm. Refrigerate leftovers.

Makes 12 servings.

One serving contains approximately: Calories 219, Fat 8g, Carbohydrates 36g, Protein 2g

Bars & Cookies

Carrot Zucchini Bars

Citrus-cream cheese frosting tops these sweet bars.

1½ cups all-purpose flour
1 teaspoon baking powder
¼ teaspoon baking soda
¼ teaspoon salt
¼ teaspoon ground ginger

2 eggs, slightly beaten
1½ cups shredded fresh carrot
1 cup shredded fresh zucchini
¾ cup brown sugar, packed
½ cup dark raisins
½ cup chopped walnuts

½ cup cooking oil
¼ cup honey
1 teaspoon pure vanilla extract

Frosting:
1 8-ounce package cream
  cheese, softened
1 cup powdered sugar
½ teaspoon vanilla extract
1 teaspoon finely shredded
  lemon or orange peel

Preheat oven to 350°.

Mix first five ingredients in a large bowl. Mix eggs, carrots, zucchini, sugar, raisins, walnuts, cooking oil, honey and 1 teaspoon vanilla extract in another bowl; add to flour mixture and stir just to combine. Spoon batter into an ungreased 13x9-inch baking pan.

Bake about 25 minutes or until a wooden pick inserted in center comes out clean. Cool completely on a wire rack.

With an electric mixer, beat cream cheese in a bowl with powdered sugar and ½ teaspoon vanilla extract until fluffy. Stir in lemon peel. Frost; cut into bars. Store in the refrigerator.

Makes 36 servings.

One serving contains approximately: Calories 125, Fat 7g, Carbohydrates 16g, Protein 2g

Cream Cheese-Frosted Walnut Pumpkin Cookies

These pumpkin cookies are sure to be a hit.

1 cup butter, softened
⅔ cup brown sugar, packed
⅓ cup granulated sugar
1 cup canned pumpkin (not pie mix)
1 egg
1 teaspoon pure vanilla extract

2 cups all-purpose flour
1½ teaspoons pumpkin pie spice
1 teaspoon baking powder
1 teaspoon baking soda

¼ teaspoon salt
1 cup chopped walnuts

Frosting:
2 cups powdered sugar
¼ cup butter, softened
1 3-ounce package cream
  cheese, softened
1 teaspoon pure vanilla extract

Preheat oven to 350°.

Beat 1 cup butter, brown sugar and granulated sugar in a large mixer bowl on medium speed until creamy. Add pumpkin, egg, and 1 teaspoon vanilla; beat until mixed.

Reduce speed to low; add flour, pumpkin pie spice, baking powder, baking soda, and salt. Beat until well mixed. Stir in walnuts.

Drop rounded teaspoonfuls of dough 2 inches apart on ungreased cookie sheets. Bake 8–10 minutes or until set. Cool completely.

Frosting: Beat all frosting ingredients in a medium bowl until smooth; cover and store in the refrigerator. Frost cookies when serving. Refrigerate leftovers.

Makes 5 dozen cookies.

One serving contains approximately: Calories 100, Fat 6g, Carbohydrates 11g, Protein 1g

Cream Cheese Pumpkin Bars

This is a perfect dessert for large groups.

4 eggs
2 cups granulated sugar
1 cup cooking oil
1 15-ounce can pumpkin puree (not pie mix)
1 teaspoon pure vanilla extract
2 cups all-purpose flour
2 teaspoons baking powder
1 teaspoon baking soda
¼ teaspoon salt
2 teaspoons ground cinnamon
½ teaspoon ground ginger
¼ teaspoon ground cloves
1 cup dark raisins

Frosting:
1 8-ounce package cream
cheese, softened
¼ cup butter, softened
2 to 3 tablespoons milk
1 teaspoon pure vanilla extract
4 cups powdered sugar
½ cup finely chopped
walnuts, optional

Preheat oven to 350°. Grease a 15x10x1-inch baking pan.

In a large bowl, beat eggs, sugar, oil, pumpkin and 1 teaspoon vanilla until smooth.

Mix flour, baking powder, baking soda, salt, cinnamon, ginger and cloves in a medium bowl; stir into pumpkin mixture. Stir in raisins. Spread batter into prepared pan. Bake 25–30 minutes or until a wooden pick inserted in center comes out clean. Cool completely in pan on a wire rack.

Frosting: Beat cream cheese, butter, milk and vanilla with an electric mixer in a medium bowl until smooth. On low speed, gradually beat in powdered sugar, 1 cup at a time, until smooth. Spread over cold bars; sprinkle with nuts. Cut 7 rows long by 7 rows wide. Store in the refrigerator.

Makes 49 bars.

One serving contains approximately: Calories 160, Fat 8g, Carbohydrates 23g, Protein 1g

Date and Pecan Pumpkin Squares

This is a wonderful treat to take along on picnics.

2½ cups whole wheat pastry flour
1½ teaspoons baking powder
¾ teaspoon ground cinnamon
½ teaspoon ground nutmeg
½ teaspoon ground cloves
½ teaspoon salt

1 teaspoon pure vanilla extract
¼ cup cold water
3 cups pitted dates,
   roughly chopped
1 cup toasted chopped pecans

1 cup plus 2 tablespoons butter, softened
1 cup light brown sugar, packed
2 large eggs
1 cup pumpkin puree (not pie mix)

Preheat oven to 350°. Grease a 13x9x2-inch baking pan.

Mix flour, baking powder, cinnamon, nutmeg, cloves and salt in a medium bowl.

Beat butter and brown sugar with an electric mixer in another bowl. Beat in eggs, one at a time. Add pumpkin, vanilla and water; beat until well mixed. Mix dates with ¼ cup of the flour mixture in a small bowl; set aside. Gradually add remaining flour mixture to pumpkin mixture. Stir in floured dates and pecans. Spread batter into prepared baking pan.

Bake about 1 hour or until a wooden pick insert in the center comes out clean. Cool in pan on a wire rack. Cut into squares. Refrigerate leftovers.

Makes 24 squares.

One serving contains approximately: Calories 240, Fat 13g, Carbohydrates 32g, Protein 3g

Frosted Pumpkin Bars

These spicy bars are great for potluck.

1½ cups all-purpose flour
1¼ cups granulated sugar
2 teaspoons baking powder
1 teaspoon baking soda
¼ teaspoon salt
2 teaspoons ground cinnamon
½ teaspoon ground ginger
¾ cup butter, melted and cooled
1 15-ounce can pumpkin (not pie mix)
3 eggs, slightly beaten

½ teaspoon pure vanilla extract
¾ cup dried sweetened
   cranberries, chopped

Frosting:
½ cup butter, melted and cool
4 cups powdered sugar
1 teaspoon pure vanilla extract
¼ cup fresh orange juice,
   approximately

Preheat oven to 350°.

Mix flour, sugar, baking powder, baking soda, salt, cinnamon and ginger in a large bowl. Stir in ¾ cup butter, pumpkin, eggs, ½ teaspoon vanilla and cranberries until well blended. Spread batter into an ungreased jelly roll baking pan. Bake 20–25 minutes or until a wooden pick inserted in the center comes out clean. Cool completely in pan on a wire rack.

Frosting: Mix ½ cup butter, powdered sugar and 1 teaspoon vanilla in a medium bowl. Stir in just enough orange juice to make a desired spreading consistency. Frost cooled bars. Cut and serve. Refrigerate leftover.

Makes 60 bars.

Variation: Use raisins instead of cranberries.

One serving contains approximately: Calories 110, Fat 4g, Carbohydrates 17g, Protein 1g

Mary Dow's Favorite Zucchini Bars

Variation: Add ½ cup chopped walnuts to batter.

⅔ cup brown sugar, packed
1 tablespoon granulated sugar
¼ cup butter or margarine
2 eggs
1 teaspoon pure vanilla extract

1 cup all-purpose flour
1 teaspoon baking soda
¾ teaspoon ground cinnamon
½ scant teaspoon ground cloves

1 cup packed unpeeled shredded
 and drained zucchini
½ cup dark raisins

Frosting:
1½ cups powdered sugar
2 tablespoons butter, softened
3 tablespoons fresh orange juice,
 or as needed
¼ teaspoon pure vanilla extract
Pinch of ground cloves

Preheat oven to 350°. Grease an 8-inch-square baking pan.

Beat sugars, butter, eggs and 1 teaspoon vanilla extract in a large bowl.

Mix flour, baking soda, cinnamon and cloves in small bowl; add to egg mixture. Stir in zucchini and raisins until well mixed; spread batter evenly in prepared baking pan.

Bake 20–25 minutes or until a wooden pick inserted in the center comes out clean. Remove from oven. Cool completely in pan on a wire rack.

Mix all frosting ingredients in a medium bowl until smooth. Frost cooled bars. Cut and serve. Refrigerate leftovers.

Makes 24 bars.

One serving contains approximately: Calories 97, Fat 5g, Carbohydrates 14g, Protein 1g

Oatmeal-Raisin-Pumpkin Cookies

My brother Nelan loves oatmeal cookies . . . so I'm sure these will become a favorite!

2 cups all-purpose flour
1⅓ cups uncooked oatmeal
1 teaspoon baking soda
1 teaspoon ground cinnamon
½ teaspoon salt

1 cup butter or margarine softened
1 cup brown sugar, packed
1 cup granulated sugar

1 cup canned pumpkin
  (not pie mix)
1 large egg
1 teaspoon pure vanilla extract
¾ cup coarsely chopped walnuts
¾ cup dark raisins

Preheat oven to 350°. Lightly grease baking sheets.

Mix together flour, oatmeal, baking soda, cinnamon and salt in a medium bowl; set aside.

Beat butter, brown sugar and granulated sugar in a large mixer bowl with an electric mixer on medium speed until light and fluffy.

Beat in pumpkin, egg and vanilla extract. Reduce speed to low and gradually beat in flour mixture until well mixed. Stir in walnuts and raisins. Drop by rounded tablespoonfuls onto prepared baking sheets.

Bake 14–16 minutes or until lightly browned and set in the centers. Cool on baking sheets for 2 minutes, then remove and cool completely on a wire rack. Refrigerate leftovers.

Makes 4 dozen cookies.

One serving contains approximately: Calories 120, Fat 5g, Carbohydrates 17g, Protein 1g

Pecan Pie Pumpkin Bars

This is a delicious dessert bar.

1 cup all-purpose flour
½ cup uncooked oatmeal
½ cup brown sugar, packed
½ cup butter or margarine, softened

¾ cup granulated sugar
1 15-ounce can pumpkin puree
  (not pie mix)
1 12-ounce can evaporated milk

2 eggs
2 teaspoons pumpkin pie spice
1 teaspoon pure vanilla extract

½ cup chopped pecans
¼ cup brown sugar, packed

Whipped cream

Preheat oven to 350°.

Mix flour, oatmeal, ½ cup brown sugar and butter in a small mixing bowl; beat on low until crumbly. Press mixture into a 13x9-inch baking pan. Bake 15 minutes.

Mix granulated sugar, pumpkin, evaporated milk, eggs, pumpkin pie spice and vanilla extract in a large mixer bowl. Beat 2 minutes; pour over baked crust. Bake 20 minutes.

Mix pecans and ¼ cup brown sugar in a small bowl. Sprinkle over filling. Bake for 15–25 minutes or until a knife inserted in the center comes out clean. Cool completely in pan on a wire rack. Cut into bars. Serve with whipped cream. Refrigerate leftovers.

Makes 12 bars.

One serving contains approximately: Calories 350, Fat 18g, Carbohydrates 43g, Protein 6g

Zucchini Brownies

Serve plain, sprinkled with powdered sugar, or frosted with chocolate frosting.

1 cup white whole wheat flour
⅓ cup baking cocoa
1¼ teaspoons baking soda
½ teaspoon coarse salt

1 cup dark chocolate chips, divided
¼ cup cooking oil
½ cup packed light brown sugar
½ cup granulated sugar
1 egg
1 egg white
1 teaspoon pure vanilla extract
1½ cups grated unpeeled fresh zucchini

Preheat oven to 350°. Grease a 9-inch-square baking pan.

Mix flour, cocoa, baking soda and salt in a medium bowl.

Melt ¾ cup chocolate chips in a large microwave-safe bowl on high for 1 minute or until smooth; cool slightly, then stir in oil, brown sugar, granulated sugar, egg, egg white and vanilla. Stir in flour mixture, then fold in zucchini. Spread batter into prepared baking pan. Sprinkle top with remaining ¼ cup morsels.

Bake about 30 minutes or until a wooden pick inserted in the center comes out just a little sticky. Cool completely in pan on a wire rack. Cut into 16 brownies. Refrigerate leftovers.

Makes 16 brownies.

One serving contains approximately: Calories 180, Fat 9g, Carbohydrates 22g, Protein 2g

Zucchini Chocolate Chip Cookies

Chocolate lovers . . . this one's for you!

1½ cups all-purpose flour
1 teaspoon ground cinnamon
½ teaspoon baking soda

½ cup butter, softened
¾ cup granulated sugar
1 large egg
1 teaspoon pure vanilla extract
1½ cups shredded fresh zucchini

1 cup uncooked quick oats
1 cup chopped walnuts
1 10-ounce package dark
   chocolate chips

Preheat oven to 350°. Lightly grease baking sheets.

Mix flour, cinnamon and baking soda in a small bowl.

Beat butter, sugar, egg and vanilla extract in a large mixing bowl. Add zucchini.
Gradually beat in flour mixture.

Stir in oats, walnuts and chocolate chips. Drop dough by rounded teaspoonfuls
2 inches apart onto prepared baking sheets.

Bake 9–11 minutes or until lightly brown around the edges. Cool on baking sheet
2 minutes, then remove from baking sheets; cool completely on a wire rack. Store
tightly covered at room temperature.

Makes 4 dozen cookies.

One serving contains approximately: Calories 80, Fat 5g, Carbohydrates 11g, Protein 1g

Jam & Jelly

Zucchini Jelly

Share a jar of this good jelly with a friend.

6 cups peeled, shredded fresh zucchini
6 cups granulated sugar
2 tablespoons fresh lemon juice
1 8-ounce can crushed pineapple, undrained

1 6-ounce package orange-flavored gelatin desert mix

Place zucchini, sugar, lemon juice and crushed pineapple, including juice, in a large saucepan. Bring mixture to boil. Cook, stirring constantly at full boil for 10 minutes.

Remove from heat. Immediately stir in gelatin until dissolved. Spoon jelly into sterilized jars. Cool on a kitchen towel. Makes about 7 pints. Store in the refrigerator.

Makes 60 2-tablespoon servings.

Variation: Use another flavor of gelatin instead of orange.

One serving contains approximately: Calories 44, Fat (trace amount), Carbohydrates 11g, Protein (trace amount)

Zucchini Pineapple Jam

Share a jar of this tasty refrigerator zucchini jam with a neighbor.

6 cups peeled, seeded, shredded fresh zucchini
6 cups granulated sugar

½ teaspoon fresh lemon zest
½ cup fresh lemon juice
1 20-ounce can crushed pineapple, undrained
1 6-ounce package strawberry-flavored gelatin dessert

Place zucchini and sugar in a large pot. Bring to a boil. Boil, stirring constantly, 6 minutes. Add lemon zest, lemon juice and pineapple; cook and stir 8 minutes. Add gelatin; stir 1 minute. Remove from heat. Skim foam. Fill clean jars, leaving ½ inch space; cool, then cover with lids. Makes about 8½ cups. Refrigerate. Store in the refrigerator up to 3 weeks.

Makes 68 2-tablespoon servings.

One serving contains approximately: Calories 84, Fat (trace amount), Carbohydrates 22g, Protein (trace amount)

Pickles & Condiments

Quick Pumpkin Butter

Spread the goodness on your breakfast toast!

1 cup canned pumpkin (not pie mix)
½ cup honey
¼ cup molasses
1 tablespoon fresh lemon juice
¾ teaspoon ground cinnamon
⅛ teaspoon ground cloves

Place all ingredients in a small saucepan. Bring mixture to a boil, stirring often. Reduce heat. Simmer uncovered until thickened, about 15 minutes. Spoon into a clean glass container and refrigerate. Chill 1 hour before serving. Makes about 1¼ cups. Store in the refrigerator.

Makes 10 2-tablespoon servings.

One serving contains approximately: Calories 79, Fat (trace amount), Carbohydrates 21g, Protein (trace amount)

Yellow Squash-Cucumber Refrigerator Pickles

Use tender yellow summer squash for best results.

4 cups thinly sliced peeled yellow squash
2 cups thinly sliced peeled cucumber
2 cups chopped yellow onion

1½ cups white vinegar
1 cup granulated sugar
½ teaspoon salt
1 teaspoon mustard seed
½ teaspoon celery seed

Place yellow squash, cucumbers and onions in a large non-reactive bowl (glass or stainless steel).

Place vinegar, sugar, salt, mustard seed and celery seed in a medium saucepan. Bring mixture to a boil. Stir constantly until sugar is just dissolved. Immediately pour mixture over vegetables in bowl; mix well. Cover bowl and place in the refrigerator. Let marinate at least 24 hours. Makes about 6 cups. Store in refrigerator.

Makes 24 ¼-cup servings.

One serving contains approximately: Calories 43, Fat (trace amount), Carbohydrates 11g, Protein (trace amount)

Zucchini Relish

This zucchini relish has a bite!

1 cup unpeeled shredded zucchini
1 cup coarsely grated yellow onion
5 teaspoons salt

2 teaspoons cornstarch
2 teaspoons ground mustard
1 teaspoon ground turmeric
1 teaspoon celery seed
1 teaspoon ground black pepper
1 cup white vinegar

½ cup finely chopped red bell pepper
1 tablespoon chopped seeded jalapeno pepper
1 teaspoon chopped seeded habanero pepper

Place zucchini, onion and salt in a large glass bowl; stir to mix well. Cover; refrigerate 8 hours. Rinse with water in a colander; drain and set aside.

In a large saucepan, mix together cornstarch, mustard, turmeric, celery seed and black pepper. Gradually stir in vinegar until blended. Stir in jalapeno pepper and habanero pepper.

Stir in drained zucchini mixture. Bring to a boil, then reduce heat and simmer, uncovered, for 30 minutes. Remove from heat; cool. Place mixture in a large non-reactive bowl. Cover and refrigerate at least 2 days before serving. Makes about 3 cups. Store in the refrigerator.

Makes 48 1-tablespoon servings.

One serving contains approximately: Calories 5, Fat (trace amount), Carbohydrates 1g, Protein (trace amount)

About the Author

Theresa Millang is a popular and versatile cookbook author. She has written successful cookbooks on muffins, brownies, pies, cookies, cheesecakes and casseroles, as well as several on Cajun cooking. She has cooked on television and contributed many recipes to food articles throughout the U.S.A.

Theresa's Other Current Cookbooks
The Best of Cajun-Creole Recipes
The Best of Chili Recipes
The Great Minnesota Hot Dish
The Joy of Apples
The Joy of Blueberries
The Joy of Cherries
The Joy of Cranberries
The Joy of Rhubarb
The Joy of Strawberries
The Joy of Peaches
The Joy of Raspberries
Cooking with Rotisserie Chicken
Salad Suppers

Theresa's Other Cookbooks
I Love Cheesecake
I Love Pies You Don't Bake
The Muffins Are Coming
The Cookies Are Coming
The Brownies Are Coming
Roux Roux Roux

Notes